Memories of Bournemouth

Part of the

Memories

series

The Publishers would like to thank the following companies for supporting the production of this book

Main Sponsor
George & Harding Limited

Bournemouth & West Hampshire Water

FA Hendy & Lennox (Holdings) Limited

George Scott & Son (Funeral Directors) Limited

First published in Great Britain by True North Books Limited
Units 3 - 5 Heathfield Industrial Park
Elland West Yorkshire
HX5 9AE
Tel. 01422 377977

ISBN 1 900463 44 X

Text, design and origination by True North Books Limited
Printed and bound by The Amadeus Press Limited

Introduction from George & Harding

Bournemouth was just beginning its transformation from barren heathland into a new town, when in the early 1860s, Charles George and Henry Harding arrived seeking work. There could not have been a better time or a better place to start a Construction Company, and George and Harding prospered and grew in size and stature with the town itself. In the intervening years, we have played our full part in the town's expansion and been responsible for the construction of literally thousands of projects, many times more than the select few highlighted in this book.

The brief history of the Company described in pages 34 - 41 concentrates by necessity on the roles played by Charles George and the Harding family in the management of the Company from the start. But Construction relies on skilled people - lots of them. It is not easy to find a computer that is clever enough to lay bricks, cut and fit the rafters of a complicated roof or hang a roll of wallpaper.

Since 1867, thousands of people, skilled craftsmen, labourers, administrators, designers and Construction Managers have worked for the Company either directly or through our sub-contractors and suppliers. They are the people responsible, who dug out the ground, laid the bricks, cut and moulded the timbers and applied the decorative finishes to create the wonderful landmarks that shaped our town and made the Company's reputation.

It is the current generation of highly skilled and experienced craftsmen and Construction Managers, working in partnership with our clients, that has made us one of the Industry Leaders in Innovation and Best Practice. Everyone is looking forward to continuing the Company's traditions into our third century of construction and continuing to play our part in the development of Bournemouth, the South of England and beyond.

We are very pleased to have been the main sponsor of this fascinating book, please enjoy reading it.

Colin Harding
Chairman

George & Harding
Construction Managers

Contents

At leisure

Who will shoe my pretty foot? This little girl only needs to use the wartime defence blocks to act as her perch. Thankfully, the German navy never tested the concrete, but, in the early years of the second world war, the south coast was always aware of the threat of invasion. In 1940, recognising that the Hampshire coast offered one of the targets for landing craft, civil defence plans included barriers, pillboxes and booms. Included in those attempts to frustrate the enemy was the deliberate damaging of the piers. Gaps were cut in them to act as a further deterrent, though the idea of stormtroopers marching down the pier seems ludicrous now. The damage done took years to undo. The main pier did not reopen until 1947.

Bournemouth did not suffer as badly as some other towns from aerial attack. Even so, the sirens whined over 1,000 times during the hostilities. In all there were some 50 raids and a total of 219 inhabitants lost their lives. The worst raids took place in November 1940 and May 1943. In the former, 53 died when parachute mines descended from the bowels of the Luftwaffe bombers. Westbourne, Alma Road and Malmesbury Park bore the brunt that night. In the 1943 raid, 77 were killed and great damage inflicted on the Metropole, Central Hotel and Beale's store. But, the little girl photographed could now look forward to the future. The war had ended and she could look for a Prince Charming to match her role as Cinderella.

Roll up, roll up for all the fun of the fair. The millennium wheel is not a patch on the times we had on a proper Ferris wheel, swingboat or the flying chairs. Stomachs turned and hearts were in mouths as we spun around, high above the heads of the others. Screams and squeals of delight filled the air. Who can forget the dodgems, when the boys crashed into the girls just to show off how tough they were? Remember the young man collecting our sixpences? Black hair slicked down with Brylcreem and long sideburns like some English Elvis, he jumped from dodgem to dodgem. Stopping only to chat up the pretty ones, he was soon off to grab the money from those on the next ride. Anyway, mum had warned us about his type. She said they were only after one thing. We didn't think she meant our tanners, but we told her not to worry. We were in more danger from the local James Dean look alike who nipped in beside us on the waltzers. When the bar dropped on our laps we were stuck with him until it stopped spinning. Still, if he forked out for a candyfloss we could put up with him until it was time to go. Dad had said to be in by 10, so we had an excuse to get away. In the meantime, let's go and try and win a goldfish in a plastic bag or knock down a coconut, if it hasn't been glued on too hard.

Above: From time to time, visiting bands would play on the bandstand below Pine Walk. Military bands, drawn from the regiments and sections of the different armed forces, gave occasional concerts. There was a high level of musicianship amongst them. Membership was a prized achievement and competition for places was fierce. In the 1930s, the competition for places in the audience was just as strong. There might have been hundreds of seats laid out, but it would not be long before they were filled. There was no such thing as reserving a place with a beach towel, as some races are accused of doing. For the British, 'bums on seats' was the way to claim your spot. Picnic in hand and a thermos in pocket, off we went, bright and early, to settle into a good vantage point. Sitting alongside us might have been a holidaymaker down from the north. He was brought up on a diet of brass bands from the collieries and factories. Well, he could just sit quietly and listen. Bournemouth could provide as good a show as any cornet blowers from Barnsley. Our backdrop was better than the grimy northern slagheaps. We had the pines that had been planted from Clifton Road to the mouth of the Bourne on the estates of Sir George Tapps. Replacing the gorse and heather that had covered the ground before, the trees softened the climate and were so picturesque; a perfect recipe for the delights about to be played to us.

Top: Every decent park or gardens had its own bandstand. The lower pleasure gardens provided no exception. Still standing today, it has heard many a stirring tune echoing out through its open shutters. In 1933, pictured from Pine Walk, the little grey squirrels that populate the area in large numbers these days were few and far between. The audience was a human one. Not many walked past along the path when the band struck up. A few lingered by the railings to hear the melodies floating out towards them. Most took up station in the scores of deck chairs on the grass and settled down for an afternoon of nostalgic entertainment. Well loved songs from Gilbert and Sullivan operettas were popular. Feet would tap to the light-hearted 'Three little maids from school' and the audience hummed along happily with 'A wandering minstrel'. Rousing sousa marches such as 'Liberty bell' and 'Washington Post' went down really well. Sometimes, the bands would show that they were really up to date and belt out their arrangements of hit songs of the day. 'The sun has got his hat on' and 'Who's afraid of the big bad wolf?' were well received. The bands would practise hard all week in school halls, above pubs or in garages big enough to accommodate them. The lucky ones had connections with factories, churches or institutions that reserved them a special room. The bandstand became their own theatre stage.

Left: Boys will be boys. Whoever coined that phrase must have been a man. Why else the excuse for either getting dirty playing football or wet through messing about in the water. A little girl would reach into the Bourne Stream to sail her boat, but one young scamp just has to take off his shoes and socks and go a-paddling. The other lads show that we are looking at a time that is lost and gone forever. In July 1933 boys had knees. You would not know it now to look at the jeans, joggers and casual trousers worn by the kids of today. The 21st century boy will never know the badge of honour that was a scabby kneecap. The school cap and short trousered uniform is a thing of the past. Even with his mucky legs, didn't the boy of that time look more presentable? At least he looked what he was - a child. It was the mums who were the ones who worried about fashion in the 30s. Their cloche hats and Bear Brand luxury stockings were the chic of the age. They are walking in the lower pleasure gardens under the backdrop of the pines that dominate the park. The fir plantation that covered this part of town had paths laid within it in 1849. The cost of clearing the brambles and laying the first walkways was £527. Money well spent.

Above: The River Bourne was formed from the confluence of two springs in Knighton Bottom and Bourne Bottom on Canford Heath. The river then ran through Bourne Chine to enter the sea at Bourne Mouth. Here the Bourne Stream runs through the lower gardens of the pleasure gardens at Westover. The gentle current of the water has always attracted children to put their paper boats onto the water and watch them drift away towards the sea. If the little lad in the centre of the frame isn't careful he will be following his vessel out into the bay. He gives every impression that he is about to go in head first. Mum will be pleased! Sir George Gervis laid out many of the buildings around here, though not the Pavilion that gazes across the gardens from the far side. The lofty pine trees that line the Bourne gave rise to the name of Pine Walk that describes the entry paths from Westover Road. The scene is timeless. Families enjoying a picnic on the grass or playing happily in the sun are scenes repeated through the years for all of us. The women in the foreground could be wearing the fashion of many eras. Perhaps the chap behind her gives a better clue. His suit and cap are straight out of 1933.

Above: The carefully tended lawns and flowerbeds of the lower pleasure gardens are a joy to behold. The bright yellows and reds of the tulips make a lovely contrast with the green of the grass and the dark hues of the trees beyond. Walking along the pathway or resting for a while on one of the park benches is a gentle way to spend a lunch hour away from the office. The opportunity to get back to nature is on hand, close to the very heart of the town. There is now a putting green in the area from where this photograph was taken. Away and behind to the left is the aviary and children's area. The chirping of the one and the happy laughter of the other helps add to the pleasures that can only come from the serenity of an English park. Under the trees there is even an opportunity to see grey squirrels at close quarters. These little creatures are so used to human beings that they merrily join in alongside the walkers. No doubt the attractions of titbits that might come their way has something to do with their friendliness. The Vistarama balloon, with its large helium bag and gondola full of up to 30 passengers at a time, now rises above this scene from its home to left of picture. How that fits with the rest of the scene is left to you, the reader, to decide.

Above right: The lower pleasure gardens are well named. Whether sitting on the benches or strolling along the paths and leafy walks within the grounds, visitors and local residents have had many hours of pleasure here since the Victorian era. Neatly laid out flower beds, the pretty bridges over the Bourne Stream and the towering pines make it a restful place to spend an hour or two away from the activity of the sea front or the hurly-burly of the town centre. Paths and promenades were developed in the gardens during the 1860s and 1870s. There were once planks placed across the Bourne for people to cross as they sniffed the perfumed air, carried down from the trees above. Three ornamental bridges replaced these basic planks in 1875. The Victorians who had come to Bournemouth for the sake of their health would have been glad of that. Those unsteady on their feet would not have relished the thought of teetering across the water on a single board. They came to Bournemouth for the application of sea water to sickly limbs, not for an all over ducking! Electric lighting was added to the gardens in 1899, making them safer and an even more popular place to walk for both the infirm and sound of body. By about 1917, the main path had its name changed from Invalids' Walk to Pine Walk. In the 1990s, an unusual addition was made to the gardens. The Vistarama balloon, nicknamed Bournemouth's 'highest attraction', had been sited in the northwest of the gardens. From its platform, it carries passengers up to 500 feet, giving them a view of 20 miles across Dorset and the Isle of Wight.

Right: Fun and games in the water for the youth of 1932. They are coming through the depression years and there is hope for a peaceful future. Their fathers fought and died in the Great War to build a better land. They could not know that in another seven years they would be promising their children the same result from the next major conflict. It was an age when the one piece bathing suit was still fashionable for men. Women had shown greater spirit in changing their swimwear in recent years. There was now little difference in the styles worn by either sex. Briefs and bikinis were two decades away. Some activities don't change. These young things were showing off, sunbathing and diving off dinghies just like the youth of today with their li-los and airbeds. In between we have had the Beach Boys and their surfing music and the growth of the water sports industry. Later in life, safety in the sea might have seen some of these young people give a thought to the work of lifeguards who are now an essential sight on the beach. More interested in saving lives than showing off muscle, the Bournemouth safety patrol saw its corps founded in 1966. The HQ at Undercliff was moved to Durley Chine in 1981. All trained in first aid techniques, there were 45 volunteers involved. In 1996 Sowster and Offshore Performance supplied a three man 85 bhp Seadoo craft. It could get from pier to pier in 90 seconds. The main centre is now at Fisherman's Walk, Southbourne, where the strong surf attracts boarders from all over the world. In late 1999, as part of a scheme to make Dorset the surfing capital of Britain, the town council paid £10,000 for a study into how to create an artificial reef out of plastic sandbags.

Below: It is obvious from this scene of west beach that Bournemouth has two climates within five yards of each other. To the south, the sun shines and it is a delight to bask in its warmth. To the north, the wind blows and there is a chill in the air. What else could explain what can be seen here? Bathing suits and swimming trunks adorn the beach as the holidaymakers soak up the sun. Up above them are the rows of folk in jackets and suits looking less than comfortable as they gaze across the sands or indulge in a little bit of knitting. In 1947 it was still expected that the more mature of us went out respectably dressed in normal daytime clothing. Ladies wore hats. It was a little racy to go around bareheaded. Men put on their sports jackets. The thought of a 50 year old dressing in jeans or shorts would have caused many an eyebrow to be raised. If the picture causes a smile today, it is as well to remember that it was only in the 1920s that the cult of sun worship had really begun. After the first world war there was something of a female revolution. The fashion of the wrapped up Edwardian had gone. The war had seen women taking on traditional male roles in factories and on the land. They were not going back to being mere servants of men ever again. They also played sports that had been just distractions for them in those earlier times. Women took to swimming, tennis and cycling - all activities meaning that parts of the body could be bared as never before. Instead of sweating on the beach, women could now strip off, within reason, and enjoy the sun.

Events of the 1930s

HOT OFF THE PRESS
The years of the 1930s saw Adolf Hitler's sickening anti-Jewish campaign echoed in the streets of Britain. On 19th October 1936 Oswald Mosley's 7,000-strong British Union of Fascists clashed head on with thousands of Jews and Communists in London, resulting in 80 people being injured in the ensuing battle. Mosley and his 'blackshirts' later rampaged through the streets beating up Jews and smashing the windows of their businesses.

GETTING AROUND
At the beginning of the decade many believed that the airship was the transport of the future. The R101 airship, however, loaded with thousands of cubic metres of hydrogen, crashed in France on its maiden flight in 1930. Forty-eight passengers and crew lost their lives. In 1937 the Hindenburg burst into flames - the entire disaster caught on camera and described by a distraught reporter. The days of the airship were numbered.

SPORTING CHANCE
In 1939 British racing driver Sir Malcolm Campbell hit the headlines when he captured the world's water-speed record for the third time in 'Bluebird' - all his cars were given the same name. A racing driver who set world speed records both on land and on water, Sir Malcolm established world land-speed records no fewer than nine times. His son Donald went on to set further records, tragically dying in 1967 when his speedboat - also named 'Bluebird' - crashed.

It took several minutes to walk the full length of Bournemouth pier. In 1932, most people came along its length to board one of the steamers that regularly called to take passengers across the bay for business or pleasure. Working class and middle class rubbed shoulders as they waiting to step onto the jetty to board the Lorna Doone, Bournemouth Queen or whichever ship was due. Men could usually be separated by their headgear. Flat caps suggested the workers. Those sporting trilbies and homburgs were more likely to be managers. The bareheaded left

us to guess. Women were less easy to classify. However, hats versus headscarves often gave a clue. The pier would give good service for many more years to come, even with a break during the war years. Some reconstruction was required in 1950 and in 1960 a theatre was added in the place where most of these people pictured were gathered. Corrosion was discovered in the original piles in 1977. A £1.7 million rebuilding programme was begun. The old structure at the shore end was demolished. A new pier entrance and leisure complex were included in the rebuilding plans. Built in an octagonal shape on two levels, the remodelled entrance was opened in 1981. Whilst residents and visitors no longer catch paddle steamers from here, the pier is still a major attraction in the resort. Unfortunately, baseball caps have replaced felt hats. Not all change is for the better.

I spy with my little eye. A lesson to us all in partnership is on show here. The direction finder has obviously spotted something of interest for her pal or little sister to focus on. This between the wars beach scene leaves plenty to the imagination. Perhaps it is the son of the famous Boscombe whale or a forerunner of Jaws that has been sighted. Perhaps not, because the girls look too happy with what they can see. It is possibly something as straightforward as picking out mum or dad splashing in and out of the shallows. These lovely children had no hang ups about what they wore. A simple sun suit or well proportioned knickers did the job. It is only in later years that youngsters seem to want to ape their elders by putting on designer swimwear and shades. Who is to blame? Is it the parents who want their offspring to grow up too quickly or the advertisers wishing to cash in? In the 30s there was no such bother. The tot doing an impression of Nelson has her hair done up properly in a ribbon. No punk cut or nose stud for her. Not much sun protection either. She might be a little pink by the end of the day. Getting a tan was becoming fashionable and Helena Rubinstein launched her famous sunburn oil to help the craze. Thoughts of ultra violet rays and skin cancers were a long way off.

Below: Striding purposefully down the beach approach from East Overcliff, this group of intrepid bathers attract admiring glances from passers by. There are all sorts of shapes and sizes to be seen in this cheery group. There is also a variety of swimming gear on view. The men are sporting the briefest of briefs, shorts and even a one piece outfit. Only the women offer some uniformity. Their suits had developed from the bloomers, black stockings and a dress with short sleeves and skirt worn by Victorians. How on earth anyone contemplated swimming in such gear is difficult to imagine. The clothing must have ballooned in the water. In about 1935 some women began to wear a two-piece suit consisting of a top and shorts. Not until the postwar period did the bikini, consisting of an abbreviated top and brief pants, come into fashion. The women pictured here are all carrying that very necessary piece of equipment, the swimming cap. Some were plain, some festooned with flowery shapes, but they were all pulled on tight to keep the salty water from frizzing the hair. Swimming had become very popular in the 1930s and had led to Hollywood careers for several top notch athletes. Johnny Weissmuller, winner of Olympic gold in 1924 and 1928, went on to play Tarzan in many films. Buster Crabbe was a gold medal winner in 1932 and played the title roles in Flash Gordon and Buck Rogers movies. Esther Williams was another fine swimmer who became a successful star, displaying her skill in several extravaganzas. Which of this Bournemouth group can you see swinging from a creeper?

Bottom: In the background the old Palace Court Hotel can be seen. The woman on the right turns her head from the camera as though she had something to hide. There was no reason to do so. This was a perfectly innocent scene from September 1947, a time when the boats and steamers had started running from the pierhead once more. After the war, the Bournemouth and Swanage service was resumed in 1946. Some of the steamers had delightful names. The Lorna Doone conjured up images of Exmoor mists and the adventures of stirring heroes and heroines. The boat was named after the famous RD Blackmore novel, written in 1869. It serviced the Isle of Wight run in the 1940s. The Bournemouth Queen served local pride. When steamer services resumed, only the east side of the pier was in use in those first days. This meant delays for passengers and captains alike. At low water only one vessel could berth at a time and people were frustrated that normal service was slow to return. This little knot of folk looks content enough. Gazing out across the choppy waters of the bay, the man in the hat could take a moment to think about those who no longer had the chance to take in the quiet scene. We were all touched by the war and memories of friends and loved ones who never returned. Perhaps he was recalling a son or brother who had been claimed by Davy Jones.

Above: Regatta week was a special time to let down your hair in 1936. For most of us, the days of the depression were not too far behind and it was good to have come through those days and enjoy life once more. The dark times had not completely gone for everyone. Hunger marchers from Jarrow would descend on the capital later in the year and fascism was rearing its ugly head across Europe. Mussolini was in Abyssinia and Spain was in the throes of civil war. But, there were good things around. Jesse Owens had swept the athletics board at the Berlin Olympics and our very own Fred Perry won Wimbledon for the third time. On west beach we could have our own mini Olympics. There were competitions and races for all to enjoy and out on the water the rowing clubs and sailing boats would be battling against each other. The beach entertainments of regatta week went back to late Victorian times. By then, those seeking pleasure rather than a health cure had flocked to Bournemouth. There was a big contrast between the vulgar and the genteel. Punch and Judy, jugglers, acrobats and minstrel shows came as a shock to the sickly, elderly and quieter set who had come to regard the town as their own. Sir George Tapps and his son, Sir George Gervis, the Christchurch MP, had worked hard in the early 19th century to create the marine village. As a haven for the well to do and those of a delicate constitution, it had few equals. Then came the swings and coconut shies and now noisy kids, enjoying themselves.

Right: The floodlit Bright's store on Gervis Pace is beautifully illuminated. As well as the portrait studios, it included the sale of artists' materials amongst its business. As a dealer in fancy goods, books and stationery it had another outlet on Old Christchurch Road. The business began in the 19th century. Fred Bright had been a missionary in India when ill health forced him to return to England. Along with many of his era, Fred came to the south coast for the benefit of his recovering strength. He was not one to rest easily. Soon he opened a needlework and wool shop in the Arcade and his business flourished from that small beginning. His son was Percy Bright, the well known stamp collector and authority on butterflies. Fred died in 1905 and his store is now called Dingles. The Arcade can be seen to the left of Bright's. It began life in 1866, on the site of the Rustic Bridge. It was designed by Henry Joy and was christened Gervis Arcade. Some unkind Bournemouth folk referred to it as 'Joy's Folly' as the rent was set at £40 per annum. The covered aspect of the Arcade was completed in 1873. Damaged by fire in 1901, it nevertheless continued to be a busy shopping area. In 1939, Drake & Co erected the modern canopy. The dome at this end of the Arcade was demolished in 1954. Major renovation was undertaken in 1986 at a cost of £250,000.

BRIGHTS

Binoculars in hand, the crowd on Bournemouth pier has an excellent view of the regatta week beach games. Down below, the marquees and deck chairs make a colourful background for the children to enjoy their sports on west beach sands. At 3.30 in the afternoon the activities are well under way. There will be winners and losers and, perhaps, a few tears. But, win, lose or draw, the children will be back next year for another try. So will the crowds. Regatta week was a popular event, as can be seen by the banks of people watching from all sorts of vantage points. The pier gave the best view. Building it had first been suggested in 1858 as a replacement for the wooden jetty that had stood there since around 1855. George Rennie was approached to design it. David Thornbury of Newcastle was authorised to build it

and work began in earnest in 1859. By 1861 the work was completed at the princely cost of £4,000. Sir George Meyrick presided at the official opening. Within its boundaries, Bournemouth once boasted three piers. Two remain today: this one and Boscombe pier, just over a mile to the east. Lovers of Boscombe pier delight in recounting the story of the 65 foot whale washed up there in 1897. Its skeleton was exhibited on the pier for five years. They should have brought it to west beach as part of the obstacle race.

Events of the 1930s

SCIENCE AND DISCOVERY

By observing the heavens, astronomers had long believed that there in the constellation of Gemini lay a new planet, so far undiscovered. They began to search for the elusive planet, and a special astronomical camera was built for the purpose. The planet Pluto was discovered by amateur astronomer Clyde Tombaugh in 1930, less than a year later.

WHAT'S ON?

In this heyday of the cinema, horrified audiences were left gasping at the sight of Fay Wray in the clutches of the giant ape in the film 'King Kong', released in 1933. Very different but just as gripping was the gutsy 1939 American Civil War romance 'Gone with the Wind'. Gable's parting words, 'Frankly, my dear, I don't give a damn' went down in history.

ROYAL WATCH

The talking point of the early 1930s was the affair of the Prince of Wales, who later became King Edward VIII, and American divorcee Wallis Simpson. Faced with a choice, Edward gave up his throne for 'the woman I love' and spent the remainder of his life in exile. Many supported him, though they might not have been as keen to do so if they had been aware of his Nazi sympathies, kept strictly under wraps at the time.

Everything comes to she who waits. Bournemouth had shown plenty of patience. The Pavilion had taken some 80 years to see the light of day, since the idea of a pagoda had been mooted. The Bournemouth visitors' directory of 1859, 70 years before the actual opening, had advocated a pavilion as an important requirement for the future of the resort. In the middle of the 20th century the Pavilion was the town's premier centre of live entertainment and crowds flocked to see the many stars who appeared on its stage. By the end of the century, the superstars were appearing at the BIC, but the Pavilion could still attract some of the second tier of personalities to tread its boards. This is a view of the main entrance, taken from Westover Road, across the edge of the lower pleasure gardens. Various building proposals were made during the early 1900s. These were either rejected or obstructed by the council or ratepayers in turn. In 1909, the council decided to erect a pavilion on the site of the Belle Vue Hotel., but, after much discussion, this scheme was thrown out. By 1922, there was another plan. Old ones were dropped and a decision made to go ahead with a different set of plans on the Belle Vue site at a cost of £100,000. In early 1923, government approval was gained. Jones and Seward were contracted to clear the site and build the superstructure. A foundation stone was laid in 1925, containing historical documents, coins and newspapers of the day. When the Pavilion opened on 19 March 1929, with Mr CT Hutchinson as manager, the cost had risen to £250,000. The first entertainer to appear was Stanley Holloway. The first musical to play here was the 'White Horse Inn', in 1933.

Above: Swimmers, it seems, want more than just a stretch of water in which to enjoy their recreation. The BIC provides a wave machine and other modern facilities that people demand today. This swimming baths once provided all that was required. Housed in this magnificent building, families spent many a happy hour, eyes red from chlorine. Here the little ones put on their water wings and paddled away with the first tentative strokes that would help them become confident swimmers of the future. Mums carefully avoided answering questions about what the 'no petting' sign meant and kept a watchful eye on the brave ones on the diving board. Way back in 1840, the Sydenham visitors' guide to Bournemouth mentioned that 'a suite of commodious warm baths has been erected contiguous to the beach'. This suite gave way to new building on the same site in 1864, becoming the Pier Approach Baths in 1888. Sir George Meyrick sold the freehold to Bournemouth Corporation for £6,000 in 1922. The baths were then purchased from the Baths Syndicate the following year. By 1934, it was decided that a new building was needed and the old one was demolished. Work began in 1935 and, by 1937, the new structure was ready for business. Designed by KMB Cross, it cost nearly £70,000. Unhappily, photographs are all that remain of this lovely piece of architecture. It was demolished in 1986 and the site became a car park, behind where the Imax cinema stands.

Top: The lower pleasure gardens, here seen in a view from the Exeter Road entrance, back on to the Pavilion and lead off towards Westover Road. Rockeries, flowerbeds, water features and shady, wooded paths make this an attractive and relaxing place to be. In 1841, Dr AB Granville suggested the laying out of the pleasure gardens on the banks of the Bourne Stream. The site was formerly known as the Meadows. A management committee oversaw the initial process that took place in the winter of 1848-9. The walkway that was completed in 1858 was at first known as Invalid's Walk. It was along this path that the Victorians women strolled, dressed in their long coats, all enveloping dresses and laced boots. Their menfolk, resplendent in top hat, high collared shirts and frockcoats, accompanied them in an effort to regain their health. On any day you could see the sickly pallor of the unwell staring out from under a bonnet or through mutton chop whiskers. As the clientele of the gardens changed, locals were happy to see the name of the walk alter to the more appealing Pine Walk. There are not many invalids to be seen in this picture. Lads, with trousers firmly anchored by their braces, practise the skills of Len Shackleton or Wilf Mannion that they have read about in Charlie Buchan's Boys' Book of Football. Mum took the opportunity to have a well earned sit down and just hope there would not be too many grass stains on those shirts for her to deal with come Monday's wash day.

Events of the 1930s

MELODY MAKERS

Throughout the 1930s a young American trombonist called Glenn Miller was making his mark in the world of music. By 1939 the Glenn Miller sound was a clear leader in the field; his clean-cut, meticulously executed arrangements of numbers such as 'A String of Pearls' and 'Moonlight Serenade' brought him fame across the world as a big-band leader. During a flight to England from Paris in 1944 Miller's plane disappeared; no wreckage was ever found.

THE WORLD AT LARGE

In India, Gandhi's peaceful protests against British rule were gathering momentum. The Salt Laws were a great bone of contention: forced to buy salt from the British government, thousands of protestors marched to the salt works, intending to take it over in the name of the Indian people. Policemen and guards attacked the marchers, but not one of them fought back. Gandhi, who earned for himself the name 'Mahatma' - Great Soul - was assassinated in 1948.

INVENTION AND TECHNOLOGY

With no driving tests or speed restrictions, 120,000 people were killed on the roads in Britain between the two world wars. In 1934 Percy Shaw, invented a safety device destined to become familiar the world over: reflecting roadstuds. In dark or foggy conditions the studs that reflected light from the car's headlights kept traffic on the 'straight and narrow' and must over the years have saved many lives.

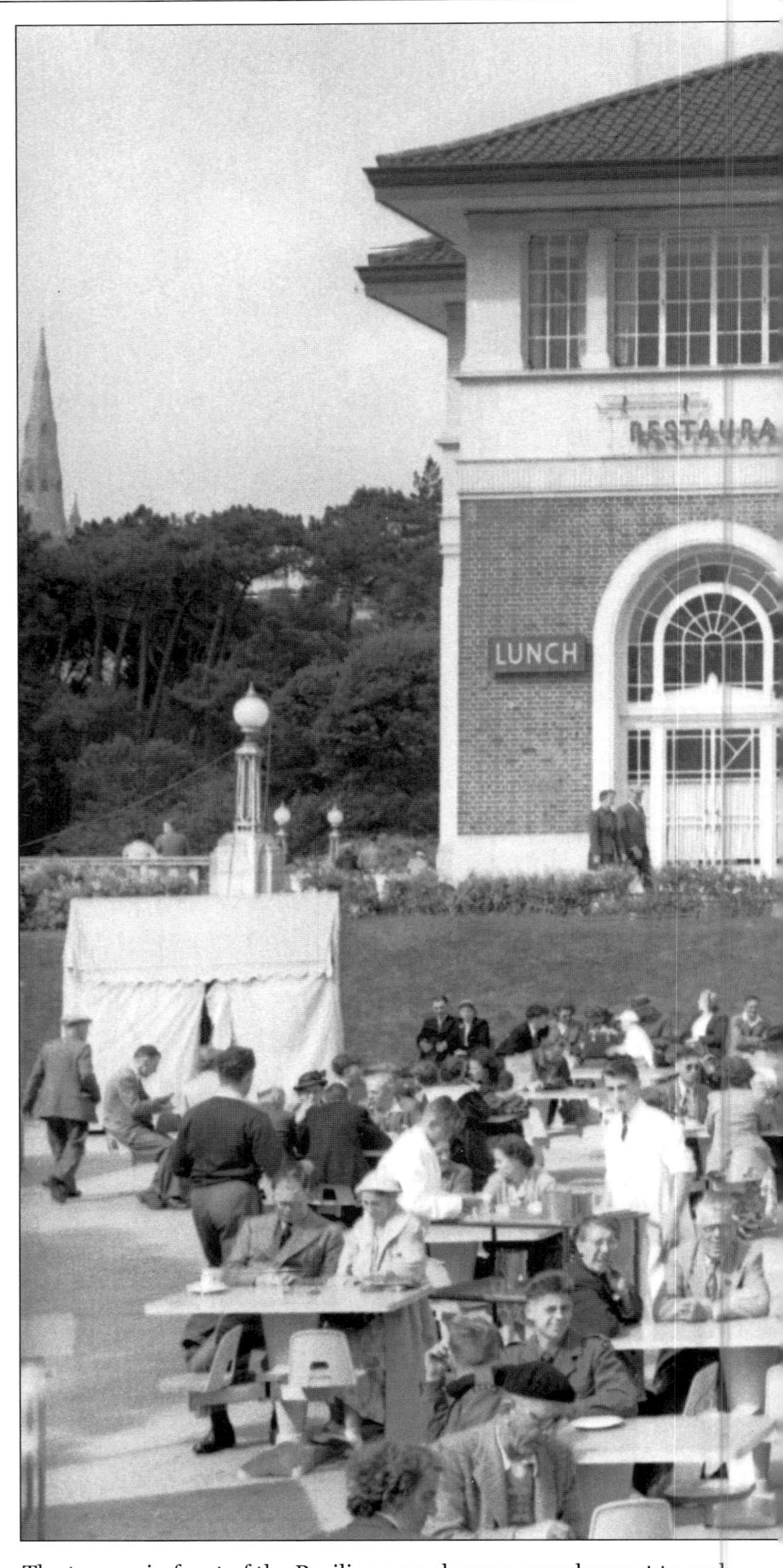

The terrace in front of the Pavilion was always a popular spot to grab a cup of tea and a fancy. If you wanted something more substantial, then a decent lunch was available to fill the inner man before that bracing walk along the cliffs. Sweethearts shared many a confidence over a plate of digestives and thanked the likes of Mr Russell Cotes for helping encourage other townspeople that this was a project Bournemouth needed. Various schemes to build a pavilion seemed to have bitten the dust by 1894, when plans had been abandoned after

much wrangling. The debate was refuelled when that much respected figure stated that a 'seaside pavilion is an absolute necessity' in one of his letters on the subject. There continued to be much argy-bargy at the time. Plans, proposals and recommendations were made. There was council discussion about the land between Belle Vue and Exeter Lane. A poll of ratepayers in 1906 rejected the scheme and the topic went backwards and forwards for nearly another quarter of a century. At long last, agreement was reached and the venture could go ahead. It almost seemed as if the town had better get it built quickly before there was another setback or change of mind. In the end, it was open for business in 1929. Henry, the Duke of Gloucester, presided at the opening ceremony. His two year old niece, Elizabeth, would later become our Queen.

The streets of change

Despite the coats worn by many of those taking a constitutional stroll, it is a bright and sunny day. The sun roof has been slipped back and the soft top rolled down. Sitting on the benches at the western end of Undercliff Drive, visitors to the town catch up on their reading. Maybe it is the latest Agatha Christie novel and the exploits of Hercule Poirot that grab their interest. Those looking at the headlines in the newspapers of the summer of 1947 will have been thrilled to read about Princess Elizabeth's engagement. She was to marry Philip Mountbatten, the son of Prince Andrew of Greece. Across the road is the entrance to the pier. It was to remain closed to the public until later in the year when repairs to its neck would be completed. The entrance seen here was demolished in 1980. In its place is a new leisure centre and show bar. There were plans submitted in 1986 to redevelop the pier approach. As happened with other plans to restructure parts of the town down through the 20th century, these seemed to take an age to get anywhere. In the 1990s further plans were submitted and, at last, some progress was made. Even so, work continued well into the next century in changing the face of this part of town. Many of the buildings at the top of the photograph have made way for the Bournemouth International Centre.

Above: This is not the Coliseum or some ancient set of Greek Doric pillars. It is a view that locals and visitors enjoyed for a long time as people used to sit here and chat away happily. Sometimes they looked along Exeter Road and up towards the Royal Bath Hotel or turned away to the right to gaze out to sea. The pillars are still on this corner that leads away to Undercliff Drive, which is where the pedestrians seem to be heading. The building to the left of the cars travelling uphill is the Rothesay Museum. Formerly the Rothesay Hotel, it opened at 11 Bath Road in 1963 as an extension of the Russell Cotes Museum. King Gustaf VI of Sweden paid it a visit in 1970. It is to be hoped it was only a coincidence that the museum closed s month later. Despite this, there was a reopening in the old Dorset and Hampshire Garage at 8 Bath Road, but it attracted an ever declining number of visitors. It closed in 1985. The view along the street is now different from this prewar one. The flyover above the pedestrian access to the seafront takes cars past what is now the Imax cinema centre. It has replaced the building on the right. The pillars are now home to the American surfers' restaurant and Hot Rocks café. The very names are a sign of the modern times. Just around the corner, to the right, you can now find the Oceanarium.

Bournemouth has a Swiss connection. Jewellery from Switzerland, that country's cuisine and the twinning of the town with Lucerne help the European flavour. Open air cafés and restaurants, weather permitting, help the continental ambience. Come to think of it, the French coastline is as near to Bournemouth as the Welsh border. Even Lucerne is the same distance from here as Aberdeen, so it is not that surprising to see more of an Alpine flavour than that of the Highlands. There is a Helvetia restaurant to the north of the town on Charminster Road, but around 1950 the Swiss Restaurant on Bourne Avenue was one of the popular places to eat out. Coming away northwest from the Square (which is anything but that shape), the man in the foreground seems very keen to examine what the couple is having for afternoon tea. Rationing was still in force for many basic as well as luxury items, so the choice was limited. However, the country was getting back on its feet and it was good to be able to repeat some of the cosier times we had before the jackboots marched across Europe. The official connection with Lucerne came in 1982. It has a number of similarities with Bournemouth. It grew to be an important town from being a little fishing village and is the centre for a busy steamer service across its lake. Sadly, the building at Hampshire Court is no longer home to the Swiss Restaurant. By the end of the 20th century it housed the Italian La Terraza.

Bottom: Pavements in posh Paris have their tables and chairs outside cafés. Parasols dot the sunny streets of Rome as Italians sup their cappuccino. Bournemouth has its Pavilion terrace. The long shadows tell us it was a lovely sunny day, perfect for summer frocks, shirtsleeves and soft drinks. Men were still very conservative in the mid 20th century. Most kept their jackets on, even if they were sweating. One chap walking across the terrace was brave enough to bare his arms. He kept his cap on, though! The germ of the idea that became the Pavilion was the work of a young architect, Benjamin Ferrey. He was commissioned to build the first villas in Bournemouth and designed the Royal Bath Hotel. Included in his plans for new buildings in the vicinity was a design for a pagoda in the pleasure gardens. It would be another 40 years before Sir George Meyrick leased the gardens to the Corporation, but this included permission to build a pavilion. The Bournemouth Improvement Act of 1892 gave the town greater powers. Authority could be sought to build a pavilion. It is just as well those seated at the tables were not waiting for that permission to be turned into reality. They would have been in for a long wait of nearly four decades for the plans to be translated into bricks and mortar. It took 80 years for Benjamin Ferrey's pagoda to become the Pavilion.

Right: This was an attractive little spot to take a seat on the bench on Alum Chine Road, Westbourne. Perhaps the three people seen here have toiled up from Alum Chine and are in need of a few minutes' rest to get some air back into their lungs and strength into their legs. Two hundred years ago, smugglers might have made a similar journey as their ran their contraband up the chines. Westbourne was just wild heathland in those days. Isaac Gulliver was one such famous villain from that age. Despite his lawbreaking, King George III gave him a measure of respectability. The 'Gentleman Smuggler' was allowed some royal licence when Gulliver told the King of a plot to assassinate him. His pistol is kept on display in the Russell Cotes Art Gallery and Museum. The chines were empty places and handy for hiding smuggled goods away from the prying eyes of the customs and excise men. Even in 1860 there were still just six houses here. The cyclist is pedalling away towards Seamoor Road. Formerly the Crescent, Seamoor Road is home to the Arcade built by Henry Joy in 1884, the year that Westbourne officially became part of Bournemouth. Gargoyles stare down from his design to keep an eye on the shoppers below. He also designed Bournemouth Arcade in the town centre. Robert Louis Stevenson Avenue is just off Seamoor Road. The famous novelist lived there in 1884-7. Whilst there he wrote 'Kidnapped' and 'Dr Jekyll and Mr Hyde'. Flats have now replaced many of Westbourne's elegant and fashionable villas.

Above: The four main tracks across the heath became the town's main roads. Eventually, they developed into Poole Road, Holdenhurst Road, Charminster Road and Wimborne Road. This last one led from Muscliff to Decoy Pond Lane, now the modern Exeter Road. Here it leads off left towards the Royal Exeter Hotel. Part of the building is the old Exeter House, built in 1811 for Lewis Tregonwell. In 1820, it was let to the Marchioness of Exeter, from whom the road took its name. The Royal Bath Hotel can be seen at the top right of the picture. Sir George Gervis opened it in 1838 on the very day that Queen Victoria's coronation took place. It was simply called the Bath Hotel. It had the 'Royal' added in 1880 when new wings were built. Further remodelling continued over the years. During the second world war it was used as a billet for the officers of the Royal Canadian Air Force. The De Vere group bought it in 1963. Despite being badly damaged by fire in 1979, it recovered its former glories. By 1990 it had been recorded by the Automobile Association as the country's best hotel. At the end of the 20th century it jealously guarded its five star status. Pedestrians and cars are now kept apart by the flyover that carries traffic on this stretch of Exeter Road down from Bath Road.

Right: Honeymooners and courting couples mingle with families and pensioners out for a stroll on the cliff path of East Overcliff Drive, high above the sands of the east beach, leading away from the town towards Boscombe. The postwar boom saw the motor car arrive in large numbers. It was an alternative to the railway as a means of getting to the seaside. Day trippers came in even greater numbers and people came in larger numbers from the north to take their annual holidays in guest houses and hotels. 'No vacancies' was a common sign in the front window of many lodgings. Bournemouth had a special attraction for newly weds. Brighton struggled to throw off its dirty weekend image, but our town had a special magic for the new Mr and Mrs. The Seychelles, Barbados and the Maldives were still light years away as honeymoon destinations. The south coast and Bournemouth, in particular, was as close to being abroad as the mill worker and bus driver in Rochdale could get. A journey to the other end of England was as a world away from the grit and grime of home. A week in Bournemouth was a memorable and mystical way to celebrate the start of wedded bliss. A brisk walk along the drive, a climb down the zig zag path to the beach and a show at the Pavilion made for a perfect day. Then it was time for bed and the moment to leave the honeymooners in privacy, but what memories they would have.

Events of the 1940s

WHAT'S ON?
In wartime Britain few families were without a wireless set. It was the most popular form of entertainment, and programmes such as ITMA, Music While You Work and Workers' Playtime provided the people with an escape from the harsh realities of bombing raids and ration books. In 1946 the BBC introduced the Light Programme, the Home Service and the Third Programme, which gave audiences a wider choice of listening.

GETTING AROUND
October 1948 saw the production of Britain's first new car designs since before the war. The Morris Minor was destined for fame as one of the most popular family cars, while the four-wheel-drive Land Rover answered the need for a British-made off-road vehicle. The country was deeply in the red, however, because of overseas debts incurred during the war. The post-war export drive that followed meant that British drivers had a long wait for their own new car.

SPORTING CHANCE
American World Heavyweight Boxing Champion Joe Louis, who first took the title back in 1937, ruled the world of boxing during the 1930s and 40s, making a name for himself as unbeatable. Time after time he successfully defended his title against all comers, finally retiring in 1948 after fighting an amazing 25 title bouts throughout his boxing career. Louis died in 1981 at the age of 67.

A delivery is being made to stock up the kiosk at the Grand Cinema. Canoodling on the back row with your boyfriend, he was not going to get as much as a warm smile if he was stingy. The least he could do was to splash out on some mint chocs or Payne's poppets. A drink on a stick in the interval was also acceptable. Girls were looked after by the lads and not expected to pay their own way. The Grand, designed by the architect HE Hawker, was built by Jones' Builders. It opened in 1922, when Valentino was

the movie heartthrob. Audiences swooned at his good looks, projected onto the screen in such epics as 'The Sheik' and 'Blood and Sand'. The cinema was bought by Savoy Cinemas in 1926, the year that the great star died from a perforated ulcer. Fans shed floods of tears. Situated on Poole Road, the Grand was one of the main entertainment centres in Westbourne. The last reel was shown in October 1975. Like so many others, it became a bingo hall. Calls of 'clickety-click' and 'Kelly's eye' do not have the same romance as holding a sweetheart's hand as the darkly handsome face of Clark Gable looked straight into a girl's heart. She could turn to her man, gaze into his eyes and imagine that he was going to sweep her away to Tara, just like in 'Gone with the Wind'. Dream on, girl.

M&G JACOBS
ILL MASON
JT 3755
DLJ 784
OGO 149

Before the war, car ownership was out of the reach of the working classes

Poole Road in Westbourne was a busy place even in the 1950s. Car ownership was becoming more popular. Before the war, it was out of reach of the working classes. The first years of peace were austere as the nation struggled to get back on its feet. Rationing continued and money was tight. But things improved as the 50s went on. It was a time of low unemployment and pay packets started to get fatter. As the prime minister, Macmillan, would later tell us in 1959, 'You've never had it so good.' As car ownership became the norm for many more people, congestion on the streets became a problem. Waiting restrictions and one way systems were brought in to help the flow. The district had grown quite rapidly in Victorian times. Many of the genteel and well off invalids who came to Bournemouth to recuperate from their illnesses liked the area and stayed. They occupied the houses that were eligible for their needs. This created a demand for more building of the same character. The neighbourhood flourished. At first, there were mainly semi-detached houses, but attractive terraces and villas soon followed. Shops opened and Westbourne buzzed with activity. The shops photographed here include the house furnishers M & G Jacobs. Further along, at 58-60 Poole Road, those who still could not afford to drive a car were able to get on their bikes from Harvey's Cycles.

Constructing a great future from an impressive past

Although the company, George and Harding Limited, as it is now known, was actually established in 1867 the origins of the business were taking root years before that date in the fledgling new town of Bournemouth.

It all began, essentially, with the birth of Charles George in 1846. Charles was born of poor parents in Corfe Mullen. His mother's name was Duke and he was later to adopt this name becoming, Charles Albert Duke George. The young Charles was orphaned and as a result became anxious to start work. He applied to the local Parish to be apprenticed to a trade. Unfortunately, Charles faced another setback in his yet young life when this request was turned down by the Parish. W J Day - one of Bournemouth's first professional photographers - who knew George in his later years, recalled that Charles was not embittered by this experience but that on the contrary it made him determined to make his own way in the world. Make his own way he did and set off to join his elder brother who was building one of the first houses on the West Cliff. They worked hard together and on Saturday evenings they would walk a journey of some ten miles back to Corfe Mullen only to walk all the way back again on Monday morning in time to start work again at six o'clock! Eventually, Charles moved to Bournemouth and worked in the yard of another builder, Edward Dyke. By this time Charles had grown to six feet tall and was good looking with a beard, fashionable at the time. These attributes probably helped him to attract Mary Miller who he later married in 1867. W J Day also recalled that, 'George and his bride drove to Christchurch Priory in a trade pony cart and on their return went back to work, she to domestic service and he to the builder's yard.' After 60 years of marriage, soon after their Diamond Wedding Anniversary, Mary died. Within six months, Charles, a practical rather than a sentimental man, had re-married, by then in his eighth decade!

It was in 1867, aged 21, that the ambitious Charles started his own building firm. He commenced business on his own account and bought a plot of land from Joseph Cooper Dean on which he built the first houses of Lansdowne Road. He let most of the houses but lived in number 29 which was located on the corner of St Paul's Lane next to the site which was to become the George and Harding works in 1873. He also built a house next to the works in St Paul's Lane for his niece on her marriage. Previously, May George, who had become Charles' adopted daughter, was living with him and his wife.

In 1883 Charles George joined forces in business with a Henry Harding to form George and Harding. Henry Harding was born in 1841 in Avon, Christchurch and began his working life as a farmhand. It is said that

***Above left:** Charles George. **Above right:** Henry Harding. **Below:** A letterhead showing the old yard in the early 1900s.*

Henry ran away from home in 1861 and shared lodgings in Madeira Vale with William Hoare and George Shears, both of whom became well known builders. Henry managed to get an apprenticeship in the building industry and eventually followed the occupation of a journeyman plasterer. He worked for Nicholas James, a builder in Holdenhurst Road who also owned a brick-works in the Kings Park area and indeed, whose daughter, Sarah, Henry later married.

Charles and Henry had actually known each other since 1867 and they had worked together in the Lansdowne area. Indeed, in 1869, they both became members of the 19th Hants Rifle Volunteer Corps and their firm became known as one of the greatest supporters the Volunteer movement in Bournemouth. Charles rose through the ranks to become a Major and then Commanding Officer of HQ Company, eventually retiring as a Lieutenant Colonel. In 1907 when the Volunteers were subsumed into the Territorial Army he was awarded the Volunteer Decoration. Henry was a Colour Sergeant for many years and was known as an active member of the shooting team.

Above: *Col George at camp in 1900.*
Top: *The company painters in the 1870s.*

Despite working together, the partnership deed between Charles and Henry was not signed until 1883, when Charles had been diagnosed as suffering from tuberculosis. His doctor had advised him that he had only six months to live but that if he went to a warm climate for the winter he may improve his chances. Therefore, Charles set off to Madeira leaving the business in Henry's capable hands. Being an inventive and resourceful man Charles spent his time in Madeira concocting a medicine to cure his lung disease. Indeed, Charles returned cured and patented his medicine as 'George's Lung Tonic'. The basic ingredient of the Tonic was Stockholm tar, used mainly for damp proofing walls. When building work was slack the medicine was prepared by labourers in the St Paul's Lane yard and sold at four shillings a bottle. This was not Charles' only invention. He also devised a method of preventing white lead paint from blistering on sills - by throwing sand on it. More notably it is said that he invented the picture rail. The story goes that a lady, for whom the firm had built a house in Meyrick Road, complained how walls were spoilt when nails were hammered into them to hang pictures. Charles suggested that to solve the problem all she had to do was, 'fix a grooved rail around the room below the cornices', make some double hooks and hang the pictures from them' and thus, the picture rail was invented. Charles also lent his talents to the

community in Bournemouth. He founded and was Chairman of the Bournemouth Working Man's Permanent Building Society which was set up to assist working people buy property and invest in savings. In 1882 he founded the Bournemouth Land Society which bought land, installed roads and services and sold the plots to George & Harding as well as other local builders. Charles also became a director of The British, Foreign and Commonwealth Lighting Control Company where the 'Gunfire switches', used to control gas and electric street lighting throughout the Empire were made.

Initially, Charles was the senior member of the partnership. However, by 1889, Henry had built up his share in the business to become an equal partner. The wages and accounts from these early years are revealing. They show that the craftsmen were paid at the rate of 6d (2.5p) an hour and the labourer 4.5d (less than 2p) and that they averaged some 53 hours work a week. Among the expenses, stocks that occur frequently, are items for candles, pig food and cabbage plants! Another item is a note of 1893 taken down at an auction sale of land on the Branksome Tower Estate. The prices of the plots sold varied from £8 to £12, which was quite reasonable for one acre plots! Amongst the contracts carried out in these early days were: the Wilts and Dorset Bank, 45 Old Christchurch Road, and on the opposite corner the Capital and Counties bank; the Head Post Office and Digby Chambers both in Post Office Road; the former Labour Exchange in Yelverton Road; the Westover corner block; The Royal Victoria Hospital, Westbourne; Borough Chambers in Firvale Road; the old Imperial Hotel at the Lansdowne which was bombed during the last war and replaced with Royal London House - now student accommodation. The firm also worked with local and London architects to construct a great many large houses, especially in the West Cliff and Branksome Park areas.

In the early 1870s, Henry Harding built the original houses in Oxford Road (which have now all been replaced by large office blocks). He and his wife lived in one of them on the north west side, backing on the firm's nursery plot, where the privet and holly hedges for the Victorian housing estates were grown. They brought up six children, four girls and two boys, all of whom were educated at the Lansdowne British School in Madeira Road. The school was demolished in the 1930s to make way for the present Police Station.

Above: The joinery shop and mill staff in 1899, including Henry's two sons, Horace Ewart (centre) and Nicholas Frank (right). ***Right:*** *An advertisement for George's Lung Tonic.*

WHY have people the misfortune to be troubled with Cancer, Tumours, painful and troublesome wounds, Chest diseases, and so many other forms of sickness?

How can these things be prevented?

I say cleanse and keep the blood pure, and nature will provide her own remedy. Shall we resort to concentrated drugs for our restoration to health? Experience convinces me that we should not. The constant use of drugs only reduce the system to a condition liable to contract any passing infectious disease. Safety and health alone lie in purity of blood, and the best and safest Blood cleanser ever known, that has successfully stood the test of the last 25 years, IS

GEORGE'S wonderful patent **Bournemouth Lung Healer and Blood Cleanser**

Sample Bottle or Pamphlet (32 pages) free on application.

Waterley Hotel, Bournemouth.

In 1895 Henry's eldest son, Horace Ewart, was apprenticed as joiner at the age of 15 and four years later his youngest son, Nicholas Frank, began his career with the firm at the age of 16. This meant that both sons were able to be present for the complete rebuilding of Branksea Castle, Brownsea Island. The Branksea Castle had been burnt to the ground in the fire of 1896. George and Harding, set to work to rebuild the castle. Painters were required to use three stage ladders in order to complete the task and so the job was advertised as needing someone with a head for heights! The rebuilding was completed two years later in 1898. This was not the only distinguished contract for the firm. Indeed, at one time the firm's letter heading boasted of being 'Contractors to the King and Queen of Sweden' as the King was convalescing in the original 'Craghead' on the Eastcliff.

The firm continued to flourish in the years preceding the first world war. This was a period of rapid development with numerous houses being built including many on the Cooper Dean Estates in the Cavendish/Dean Park Road, West Cliff and Charminster areas, Boscombe Cliffs and the Branksome Park Estate. Contracts as far a field as London, Lyndhurst, Thames Ditton, Weymouth and Salisbury were carried out, as well as a large amount of Repair and Maintenance work. The terrace of shops in Holdenhurst Road, opposite the Drill Hall, were built to be let and remained the firm's property until 1915. The whole of Corporation and Lytton Roads were developed and further contracts such as the Bournemouth School (in Porchester Road, since demolished), Hawthorn's Hotel (now the Wessex Hotel) and the Savoy Hotel were completed. Edgar Barrow, who was an apprentice of the

__Above:__ Wilts & Dorset Bank, 45 Old Christchurch Road in 1878. __Left:__ The Savoy Hotel, West Cliff under construction in 1906. __Below:__ The joinery mill in 1900.

firm in the joiner's shop, recalled working on fittings for the new Wilts and Dorset bank at Boscombe in 1901 and the oak staircase for Branksea Castle three years previously. Another job in progress at the same time was the joinery for Michelgrove House, Boscombe. The windows and doors of the house were done in teak and the staircase was completed in walnut with elaborate detail.

Working far away from the headquarters was not always an advantage. Indeed, in 1900 a job was carried out at Thames Ditton designed by Sydney Tugwell, a well known Bournemouth architect. This involved a large amount of joinery in Austrian oak in the classical style. This however, was not the problem. The doubts occurred when a rumour reached Henry Harding that the men were taking advantage of being far away from the headquarters and were not starting work at the prescribed time of six o'clock in the morning. Henry decided to find out for himself if the rumours were true. One Sunday evening he left Bournemouth on the mail train, arriving at Waterloo at quarter past four in the morning. He eventually arrived on the job at quarter past six only to find everyone working hard. He never did discover who gave them the tip-off!

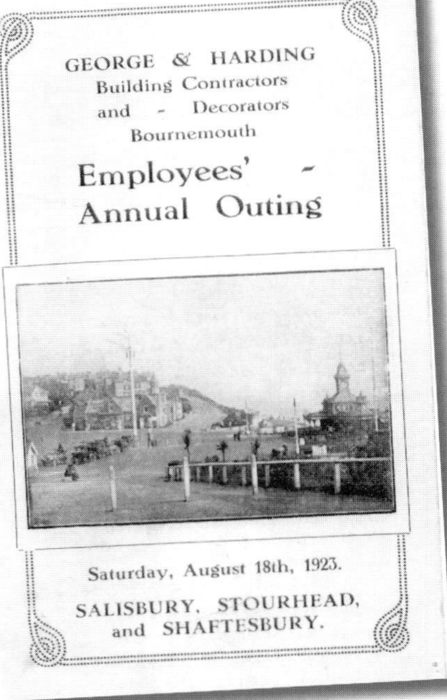

GEORGE & HARDING
Building Contractors
and - Decorators
Bournemouth

Employees' - Annual Outing

Saturday, August 18th, 1923.
SALISBURY, STOURHEAD, and SHAFTESBURY.

The firm carried out a considerable amount of work for the Bournemouth Gas and Water Company, including their offices and showrooms on Poole Hill and many of the original buildings at Longham, Surrey Road and Wallisdown. However, it became a policy of the firm not to tender for Local Authority contracts. This policy was upheld from 1885 until after the first world war due to the fact that Charles was a member of the Bournemouth Commissioners. Also, when the town was given its charter, he became a member of the Council and within a few months was elected as one of the town's first Aldermen. This policy was re-established in 1932 when Henry's son Horace became a Councillor.

At the outbreak of the first world war, during the year between 1913 and 1914, the Miramar Hotel was in a state of ongoing construction by the firm. However, the owner of the hotel was a German National and on the 4th of August when war was declared he disappeared. This led rise to the suspicion that he was a spy! Throughout the duration of the war however, little or no new construction was carried out by the firm. Just as the war was entering a difficult stage these unhappy times were compounded, in 1915, with the death of Henry Harding at the age of 74. Henry's obituary remembered him not only for the large number of buildings he was respon-

Above: *Notice of the employees' annual outing in August 1923...* ***Top:*** *...and the outing itself with Nicholas Frank Harding sitting on the runningboard outside the family home in Oxford Road.*

sible for but as one of the oldest members of the 'Loyal Bourne Lodge of Oddfellows', a contributor to the 'Hospital Saturday and Sunday Fund from its commencement' and a 'seatholder at the East Cliff Congregational Church'. His funeral was held at Wimborne Road cemetery in Bournemouth with a 'large and representative attendance'.

A new partnership was formed on Henry's death between Charles George, Horace Ewart and Nicholas Frank Harding, together with W L Winship, the Chief Estimator and W R Osborne, the Property Manager. This uneasy partnership survived until the end of 1932 when the three older men eventually retired. When the original partnership deed was signed in 1883, it stated that Charles George and Henry Harding would each draw £5 each week as a salary. Any surplus profit at the end of each year was to be divided equally but to be retained by the firm in the form of investment property. So every winter, when work slackened off, the company built houses to rent, blocks of shops, such as the terrace in Holdenhurst Road from the Lansdowne up to the old Fire Station as well as hotels. The Waverley Hotel near Central Station has been demolished for the roundabout by Abbey Life, but the old Vale Royal Hotel, opposite the BIC in Exeter Road is still being used as the Adult Education Centre. Both hotels were run by the firm as temperance hotels following Charles and later, Horace Harding's evangelical temperance beliefs. It has to be said that Henry Harding and his son, Nicholas Frank, happily made up for their partners' aversion to alcohol stimulation.

Like many wealthy self-made men, Charles George didn't like parting with his hard earned money. When Henry died he claimed that some of the joint property, including the valuable Vale Royal Hotel, were his personal assets. Although Horace Ewart eventually conceded this, and other claims, the new partnership was never easy, particularly when in the latter stages Charles George would appear on site to interfere - when he was in his late eighties.

At the close of the war business was resumed as usual and the 20s brought with them another period of development. The employees were treated every year to an annual outing. The outing of 1923 comprised of a full day of events including: a visit to Salisbury Cathedral; dinner at The Spread Eagle Hotel in Stourhead; a Tug of War and other sporting events at King Alfred's Tower; tea and presentations at Cosy Corner Restaurant; a visit to Iwerne Model Village; and finally back to Bournemouth for a fireworks display. The lavish outings were discontinued in the late 20s, when after a raucous boat trip on the River Thames, several employees were arrested in Reading. Notable contracts of the period included: extensions to Lytchett Heath for Lord Rockley; extension to the Highcliffe Hotel; the building of St Warburga's School in Malvern Road and a lecture hall for Bournemouth Natural Science Society in Christchurch Road.

The 30s were times of change for the business. In 1931 Nicholas Frank's son, Henry John Harding, joined the firm. A year later, at the age of 90 Charles George retired along with Winship and Osborne. Consequently, Nicholas and Horace bought the business , setting up a new partnership. In 1933, Horace's son Ronald joined the firm

Below: *Mr George's house, 29 Lansdowne Road pictured in 1967. The houses have since been demolished and the site is now student accommodation.*

after gaining one of the first Higher National Diplomas from the Brixton School of Building and serving a year with Y J Lovell and Son of Gerrards Cross. Years later another generation of Hardings, Rufus, was to attend South Bank University, formerly the Brixton School and coincidentally, his brother, Magnus also trained with Y J Lovell! In 1937, Horace's daughter, Kathleen, joined the family firm to become the first female member of staff in the business.

It was also during the 1930s that Henry John and Ronald Harding were enlisted to save the Joinery Mill from burning down. Fred James, the firm's carter, who lived on the premises to tend the horses, noticed smoke coming from the floor duct where the exhaust from the gas engine that powered the machines passed through to the outside wall. Instead of calling the Fire Brigade (George & Harding were one of the original subscribers to Bournemouth's telephone system with the number Bournemouth 25), Fred rode one of the horses down to King's Park where the George & Harding cricket team were playing. The whole team rushed back to help, still in their 'whites'. Fortunately, another one of Charles George's innovations, a large tank of water fed by rainwater, once used to feed the original steam engine, provided enough water to extinguish the fire and save the day.

Notable contracts in the 30s were the parade of shops and flats on Pokesdown Hill, followed quickly by flats higher up the hill, Marlborough and Huntley Mansions with one of Ronald's uncles, William Fox of Fox & Sons the Estate Agents. Also many large private houses were constructed, such as Yaffle Hill, Broadstone, for Cyril Carter of Carter's Tiles, and a magnificent cliff top house in Sandbourne Road, now owned by Max Bygraves.

During the second world war, the firm concentrated on war work, including sea defences, gun emplacements and pill boxes. These included the famous camouflaged one in Southbourne, designed to look like an Estate Agent's office with the letter box serving as the gun port. After the war the firm concentrated on Repair and Maintenance and extensions for a wide range of private and commercial clients.

Nicholas Frank died in 1958 and in 1961 the firm was incorporated as George & Harding Limited with Ronald as Managing Director and his father Horace Ewart and sister Kathleen as Directors. Horace died in 1964 and Ronald's son Colin returned from studying Construction Management at Manchester University a year later to join the Company as Joint Managing Director at the age of 24.

Top: *The staff at the time of the company's centenary in 1967.*
Above: *The office staff in 1951. From left to right: Ronald Harding, Dick Toms, Nicholas Frank Harding, Kathleen Harding, Joan Hutton.*

Having acquired the local companies of H J Hillman, F Grant, J Leeming & Sons and later A S Prince and E W Kingsbury, the Company embarked on a course of steady expansion. Many local branches of Lloyds and National Westminster Banks and Boots were refurbished in the 1970s and 1980s.

Expansion continued with the establishment of the separate companies of George & Harding Dorchester, Butchers of Warminster and Gildea & Harding based in Warwick, extending the area of operation and the range of regular clients, now including Local Authorities and other public sector bodies.

In the 30 odd years since George & Harding's Centenary celebrations in 1967, the Company has constructed over 50 new schools, major school extension or college and University projects, numerous factories including those on the Yeomans Road Estate and many refurbishments for the TSB and Midland Banks. The Company has constructed around 50 Little Chefs throughout the South and Midlands, and completed many major contracts for local hospitals and medical centres. Increasing emphasis is being placed on specialist refurbishment at places as far afield as Warwick Castle, Longleat House and the Tilford Institute in Surrey, the Edwardian Architect Edward Lutyens' first commission, built in 1898. Between 1976 and 1990, George & Harding completely rebuilt the Lansdowne (now the Nuffield) Hospital in Lansdowne Road and have constructed hundreds of social housing units for local housing associations.

Colin Harding became Chairman in 1985 and has pursued a policy of continuous improvement and innovation to enable the Company to weather recessions and the rapidly changing markets of construction. A graduate only management recruitment policy was introduced in the early 90's and most senior executive functions are now carried out by this up and coming group of professional Construction Managers, including Colin's sons, Magnus and Rufus.

The Company and its Directors have played their full part in the development of Bournemouth and the Construction Industry nationally. Mr. George was a Town Commissioner and Alderman, Horace Ewart Harding a Bournemouth Councillor and Ronald a Poole Justice of the Peace. Colin has been involved in the development of numerous national initiatives for the Construction Confederation and Government since 1979 and was President of The Chartered Institute of Building in 1994/95.

George & Harding is a founder member of the Chartered Building Company Scheme, which identifies those companies whose Directors are professionally qualified and who 'discharge their duty to their clients with honesty, efficiency and integrity'.

At Charles George's funeral in 1938 the Minister said that 'Colonel George's character was marked not only by a certain ruggedness but also by uprightness and integrity'. Indeed, as the Company moves into its third century of trading, Charles George and Henry Harding would be very satisfied with the way their business has progressed, recognising the honest, efficient and innovative policies that still flourish.

Above: *The Lansdowne Nuffield Hospital.*
Below: *The Learning Resource Centre of Bournemouth & Poole College of Art.*

Down on the beach!

Looking along Undercliff Drive towards Bournemouth pier, the east beach is filling up with sun worshippers on holiday or down for the day from Salisbury, Winchester and Newbury. People have piled off the train or driven down the A338 or A31 to get here. They won't be disappointed. Miles of golden sand await them here and on the other side of the pier on the west beach. Men hiring out deck chairs rub their hands with glee at another day of brisk business. The continental package holiday was some time away. The British seaside and its traditional attractions of simple amusement arcades, cricket on the beach, donkey rides and the creation of magnificent sand castles was pleasure enough for us. Part of the pier had been blown up in 1940 as a precaution against enemy invasion and remained closed for the duration. The clock on the roof of the pier entrance had been damaged by a blast in 1941. It was boarded up and the clock removed, being restored in 1946. The BIC has replaced the houses beyond the pier entrance on the corner of West Cliff Promenade. For some families this was one of the first holidays together since the war as servicemen returned from duty overseas. It was a time for young children to get to know fathers of whom they had seen little in preceding years. Wives had to adjust from a life as a single parent and men had to relearn the art of being husbands rather than bachelors.

In the distance, Canford Cliffs curve round towards the Sandbanks and Poole harbour. Many a good walk has been had along the beach or cliff top since Lewis Tregonwell, acknowledged as Bournemouth's founder, first came to the area. Here we are looking from a spot close to where the modern Imax stands, with the Oceanarium to the right. Britons have always been good walkers. Any summer day will see folk taking the air along the several promenades that make up Bournemouth sea front. Lovers stroll hand in hand along the cliff tops of East Overcliff or down the zig zag paths that bring them from there to the beach. It was just the same in 1936. This may not have been the best day of the summer, but we could still enjoy our visit to the seaside. Men put on their trilbies or flat caps, depending upon their social rank, and accompanied their wives on the casual stroll along the front. Some of the better off women used the occasion to show off their fur coats, but no one minded. Everyone could enjoy the day, whatever his station. The town's popularity had rocketed in the half century before this photograph was taken. Sea bathing had become fashionable and the population expanding to a degree that the integration of services such as water, sanitation and lighting had been a problem. The individual estate and land owners controlled them. There was no municipal government until the 1856 Bournemouth Improvement Act, but this helped change a pretty spa into a town and by 1890 it had gained its own identity.

Above: To within about 30 miles, you know just where you are when you hear the word 'chine'. Other than Hampshire, Dorset or the Isle of Wight the word does not appear in a place name anywhere else in Britain. It is an oddity of the English language that such an archaic word should have remained in regular use in this one part the country. It is derived from the old English word 'cinu' and means a rock cleft or ravine. Some locals have an even more unusual name for this feature. They call it a 'bunny'. Taken from the clifftop this is a view of Middle Chine, taken in the 1940s. The best known chines along this stretch of coast are Alum Chine and Durley Chine. The former shares part of its name with Alum Bay on the Isle of Wight, famous for its many coloured sandstone cliffs. The derivation of the name Durley Chine is open to argument. Some think it comes from the old English for 'deer wood', but the truth is probably more simple and less poetic. William Dean, a 19th century landowner, is thought to have named the area after the Durley that is near Bishop's Waltham, from where his family came. The beach huts along the shore line have long been a feature of the Bournemouth coast. Possession of one is a jealously guarded jewel. The beach office now rents them out on a daily or weekly basis. They have their own stoves, chairs and dinky curtains.

Top: When peace came to Britain after World War II it was time to pick up the threads of normal life once more. What could be more typically British than to spend a day at the seaside? Like the man who broke the bank at Monte Carlo, we could 'stroll along the prom with an independent air.' Hitler had been beaten, the war with Japan was behind us and the new Labour government offered the hope of the welfare state. We were free to choose where we went without wartime restrictions. What better place to come than the sea front and the pier. There we could chat about the glorious summer of 1947 when Denis Compton scored a hatful of runs and of the 1948 Ashes series that saw Bradman's last visit to this country. The pier had seen some changes in its life. The wooden one that was opened in 1861 had been badly damaged by the gales of 1867 and 1876. The leading pier designer, Eugenius Birch, was brought in to plan out a replacement. Iron was the material of the 19th century. Great bridge builders like Telford and Brunel had led the way. Birch's iron pier was opened to the public in 1880. The Lord Mayor of London cut the ceremonial ribbon on a pier that was 845 feet in length. Later it was extended to 1,000 feet. The Duke of Argyll opened a sister pier at Boscombe in 1899.

It was the coming of the railway in 1870 that helped transform the town from a sleepy village into the busy resort it is today. Many of the first visitors came to sample the pine scented air. The gentle perfumes and quiet of the environment attracted ailing Victorians to try the cures of seawater in attractive surroundings. Rubbing saltwater onto sick bodies was supposed to help recovery from a number of afflictions. Tuberculosis was a big killer in those days. Several sanatoria were built to treat the invalids. Seawater was even drunk as a cure. Some doctors recommended that small amounts taken internally would be of benefit to the digestion. The railway brought something that was not easy for the first residents to digest. It was the common man. Just a trickle came at first, but the 1871 census saw that the village was home to over 6,500. By the turn of the century the population explosion resulted in 60,000 calling Bournemouth home. Trains brought many thousands more on day trips or holidays during the summer months of the early 20th century. On a bank holiday, such as this one in 1936, west beach and other sandy stretches of the then

Hampshire coastline were black with people, packed like sardines and enjoying the sun, sea and salty air. Little boats bobbed on the water and children happily put little flags on top of the miniature Windsor Castles they had built. They buried mum's legs in the sand and dad, knotted hankie on head, dozed contentedly on his deckchair. This was the year that saw three British kings on the throne. On the death of George V, his son, Edward VIII, succeeded to the throne. However, he had abdicated by the end of the year following the concern about his involvement with the American, Mrs Simpson. His brother, George VI became the monarch and things returned to normal.

Events of the 1940s

HOT OFF THE PRESS

At the end of World War II in 1945 the Allies had their first sight of the unspeakable horrors of the Nazi extermination camps they had only heard of until then. In January, 4,000 emaciated prisoners more dead than alive were liberated by the Russians from Auschwitz in Poland, where three million people, most of them Jews,were murdered. The following year 23 prominent Nazis faced justice at Nuremberg; 12 of them were sentenced to death for crimes against humanity.

THE WORLD AT LARGE

The desert area of Alamogordo in New Mexico was the scene of the first atomic bomb detonation on July 16, 1945. With an explosive power equal to more than 15,000 tons of TNT, the flash could be seen 180 miles away. President Truman judged that the bomb could secure victory over Japan with far less loss of US lives than a conventional invasion, and on 6th August the first of the new weapons was dropped on Hiroshima. Around 80,000 people died.

ROYAL WATCH

By the end of World War II, the 19-year-old Princess Elizabeth and her distant cousin Lieutenant Philip Mountbatten RN were already in love. The King and Queen approved of Elizabeth's choice of husband, though they realised that she was rather young and had not mixed with many other young men. The engagement announcement was postponed until the Princess had spent four months on tour in Africa. The couple's wedding on 20th November 1947 was a glittering occasion - the first royal pageantry since before the war.

Above: Everything that you wanted from a seaside holiday in 1936 was to be found around west beach. Lads and dads rolled up their trouser legs and mums and little girls hitched up their skirts to dip toes into the salty waters of Poole Bay. Buckets were filled, holes dug in the sand and fine castles sprang up along the beach. Budding Bradmans and Hammonds practised their cover drives on a soggy ball sent down by granddad. The less energetic sat around, catching up on their reading or napping quietly. Above them lay the hotels and guest-houses of West Cliff. Landladies, who could reduce a grown man to ashes with just one look, ruled many of these with rods of iron. All he had to do was be five minutes late for the evening meal. The impressive Bournemouth International Centre, the home to political party conferences and many other activities, has now replaced those buildings to the right. Lewis Tregonwell, recognised as the founder of the town, would not recognise the place. He is given pride of place in the history of Bournemouth. A statue to this former Dorset Rangers captain, sculpted by Jonathan Sells, stands in the BIC grounds. CC Creeke, who is known, quaintly, as the first town surveyor and inspector of nuisances, designed it! The statue is also dedicated to the memory of Bournemouth's three winners of the Victoria Cross.

Above right: Picture postcards and photographs of seaside resorts always show golden beaches, azure seas and sun streaming down from a cloudless blue sky. Yet, this wintry scene is just as attractive as any bright August day and so much more peaceful and romantic. Gone are the trippers and candyfloss eaters. What remains is a chance to get some isolation to enjoy the shore line on a day when you are unlikely to see more than a handful of others. An English seaside town in January is like no other. There is salt in the air and the spray in your face as the sea is whipped up on the winter breeze. The crunch of the snow underneath warm boots is the only sound to compete with the cry of the hardy gulls that have stayed at home for the winter. People used to seeing the beaches and promenades covered with heaving bodies can gain so much pleasure from having that whole stretch of coast to themselves. Instead of the hustle and bustle and rugby scrum of the holiday crowds, there is now the bleak emptiness of a scene that, but for the beach huts, was just as nature intended. Strip away the shelters, huts and lampposts and here is the land that first attracted Captain Tregonwell and his bride, Henrietta, to make this place their home, nearly 200 years ago. Take in the view and the history and then it is back home to a roaring fire and a warming cup of cocoa.

Below: Quite a complicated way of getting into the water, don't you think? Has no one told these 1932 bathers that you can wade out into the sea much more easily? Men's 'cossies' were more modest than those worn by women, it seemed. Quite why the male chest had to be covered remains a mystery. From this scene it can be gathered that the dip in the sea was still a fairly new idea. There are very few who have hazarded out of their depth beyond the first wave of breakers. Swimmers of the time were more usually paddlers and splashers, which is why the sea slide gave that little sense of adventure to those about to launch themselves into the surf. Children made good use of old innertubes and tyres as swimming aids. The majority had still to learn the art of the doggie paddle and breaststroke because school swimming lessons were few and far between. It was not that long ago that bathing machines had been wheeled out across the sand and their owners entered the water inside the privacy of large tent-like contraptions. By the time this picture was taken Bournemouth, like Bognor, New Brighton and Blackpool, was becoming the site of seaside speculation. Beach huts and seafront businesses were springing up as the commercially minded saw that this type of holiday was here to stay. Let us hope that those on the steps timed their slide to coincide with an incoming wave. Otherwise, an undignified and sandy landing was coming their way.

Bottom: Wish you were here on west beach. Wish you were here instead of us, perhaps. Thousands of not so jolly holidaymakers sit well wrapped against the chilly breeze that was the summer of 1936. Umbrellas acted as windbreaks and trilbies were well pulled down to keep out the wind. Coats remained tightly buttoned and rugs were pulled up over blue knees. Despite this, we stayed. The British are a hardy race. It took more than a gust of wind to shift them from the little stretch of sand they had claimed as their own. Not only that, these deck chairs had been rented for the day and we were blowed if we didn't get our money's worth. By this time some 13 million workers received paid holidays, a far cry from the employment conditions of their parents. They were not going to waste this benefit by going indoors. The beach entertainers had been driven away by local regulations, but there were still donkey rides to be had and the stop me and buy one ice cream sellers around, even in this weather. These sights, repeated up and down the country, were the inspiration for Donald McGill's saucy postcards. The people also provided the likes of Billy Butlin with the recipe for success. Before long, many of those suffering here would be attracted to the 'morning campers' cry of the holiday camp, with its guaranteed entertainment. Butlin, who had made a pile from amusement parks, established his first camp at Skegness in the same year as this photograph was taken. The redcoats would soon take over the holiday organisation of many pictured that raw day.

Events of the 1940s

MELODY MAKERS

The songs of radio personalities such as Bing Crosby and Vera Lynn were whistled, sung and hummed everywhere during the 1940s. The 'forces' sweetheart' brought hope to war-torn Britain with 'When the Lights go on Again', while the popular crooner's 'White Christmas' is still played around Christmas time even today. Who can forget songs like 'People Will Say we're in Love', 'Don't Fence Me In', 'Zip-a-dee-doo-dah', and 'Riders in the Sky'?

INVENTION AND TECHNOLOGY

Inspired by quick-drying printers' ink, in 1945 Hungarian journalist Laszlo Biro developed a ballpoint pen which released viscous ink from its own reservoir as the writer moved the pen across the page. An American inventor was working on a similar idea at the same time, but it was Biro's name that stuck. A few years later Baron Bich developed a low cost version of the pen, and the 'Bic' ballpoint went on sale in France in 1953.

SCIENCE AND DISCOVERY

In 1943 Ukrainian-born biochemist Selman Abraham Waksman made a significant discovery. While studying organisms found in soil he discovered an antibiotic (a name Waksman himself coined) which was later found to be the very first effective treatment for tuberculosis. A major killer for thousands of years, even the writings of the ancient Egyptians contain stories of people suffering from tuberculosis. Waksman's development of streptomycin brought him the 1952 Nobel Prize for Medicine.

Away to the west lie Canford Cliffs and, before there, Durley and Alum Chines. Dogs are allowed on the latter's wide and sandy stretches, which can be described as a 'bone' of contention, these days. Nearby Durley has the prestigious Blue Flag award, the sign of a top class beach. Southbourne, a few miles to the east, also proudly boasts the same award at Fisherman's Walk, which is also listed in the Good Beach Guide. Back in the late 1940s, however, there was no real thought that beaches might need to be graded for health reasons. The only problems we

might have found were from unexploded bombs or mines being washed up. We took our litter home in those days and did not leave coke cans and polystyrene burger trays all over the place. The trouble was we were not aware of the level of sewage and other horrors that might be floating around out there. To be fair, there had not been long for problems to grow up. The beach holiday was still a recent thing. It was only towards the end of the 1920s that the first women's swimsuits appeared without a skirt attachment. Only then did the children realise that mum had legs. It was only as recently as 1903 that the first Alpine TB clinic had opened, using sunshine as one of its main treatments. The wealthy had long gone to the Riviera for the winter and some began to risk the summer heat as well. Those with less cash to spare copied them by coming to the English Riviera and a new mass holiday fashion was born.

Above: People came to Bournemouth to recuperate, refresh their weary bodies and rest their tired bones. That was in the 19th and early 20th century. When Queen Victoria was on the throne, people flocked here to take the waters and enjoy the pleasant climate, away from the harsh environment of the smoky industrial revolution. So much so, the local paper complained that the number of invalids was threatening to outnumber other visitors. Bournemouth was in danger of becoming a metropolis of bath chairs. By the middle of the 20th century, people still poured into the town on bank holidays and in high summer. They were here to refresh their weary bodies like their ancestors had done. But, theirs was not a visit born of illness. Their frames were tired from the daily grind and not worn out by disease or poor living conditions. Deck chairs replaced the bath chairs and a fortnight of fun by the sea was there to be enjoyed. The scene has changed little, over 50 years later. The sea front buildings still stand on west beach and the flags wave just as gaily. Amusement arcades and cafés provide alternatives to sitting on the beach. The cliffs and chines continue to attract visitors to walk the paths above the beaches or to stay on the sands and lap up the sense of peace that is an English beach holiday.

Right: It is the summer of 1947 and, whatever the weather, we are going to the seaside to enjoy the beach. Coats, hats and shoes lie scattered in some cases, but are generally being kept on as the British grit their teeth and work at enjoying their holiday. There must be something in our genes that says a holiday means going to sit on the sand. Never mind that the day is chilly or windy. It's out with the bucket and spade, pull up the deck chair and sit there staring at the sea. It is almost as if we are daring the weather to drive us away. King Canute had the same idea when he looked at the tide and ordered it back. In the distance, the coastline swings in a broad sweep out past Boscombe and Southbourne to Hengistbury Head at the start of Christchurch Bay. For much of its length crowds thronged the beaches and dared the elements to force them off. They had good reason to stay. Holidays and relaxation were to be treasured. The war had not been long gone and people could recall the anxious looks at the sky they had been making for so many years. What better place to come than normally sunny Bournemouth? A good time was virtually guaranteed. It had been recognised as a special place for about a century. In his book, 'Spas of England and Principal Sea Bathing Places', written in the early Victorian era, Dr Granville wrote 'I look on Bournemouth and its yet unformed colony as a perfect discovery among the sea nooks one longs to have for a real invalid.' By 1947 the colony was large with few invalids in sight, just those sick of the weather.

Events & occasions

A row of pretty girls parade their charms for the judges, and in spite of the happy smiles, 17 hearts must have been beating nineteen to the dozen as the girls waited nervously to hear their decision.
The dresses of the contestants in the Bournemouth Regatta Queen contest reflect the fashion of the day, when narrow waists and mid calf length, widely flared skirts were the 'in thing', together with the short, soft perm and Louis heels. Remember paper nylon underskirts? And those frothy net ones? Lady readers who were in their teens and twenties during the 1950s certainly will. Immensely feminine, the crisp petticoats transformed a loosely hanging skirt into a mini 'crinoline' that rustled seductively as they walked. And perhaps our male readers will remember with nostalgia those occasional tantalising glimpses of foaming petticoat! Note also that some of these girls are wearing gloves, at the time an essential accessory to the well-dressed young lady's outfit. This kind of competition was to eventually find itself a victim of 'political incorrectness' as the women's libbers symbolically burnt their bras and declared beauty contests to be demeaning to women - though beauty contests began to make a comeback towards the end of the 1990s.

Above: In the late 40s and early 50s, bathing suits were becoming that bit more revealing than the swimwear of before the war. They were still a mile away from the topless styles and the thongs that appeared later in the 20th century, but change was on the way. The first bikinis made an appearance on British beaches. It is no coincidence that the two piece wearer is perhaps the youngest woman pictured here. The youth revolution was on the way. Fashion and music, within a few years, would be geared to the young. Crooners went and rockers came in. The teenager was born. These women, amongst Bournemouth's prettiest, were competing in the 'How do you shape?' beauty contest. Most entered for fun, but for one or two there might have been thoughts of further glories. There was money to be won and prestige to be gained if you went on to be 'Miss Bournemouth' or Miss Great Britain'. Girls could dream of going on to meet Eric and Julia Morley, organisers of the Miss World contest. They would practise swinging their hips and being able to say that their ambition was to travel the world. All contestants seemed to want to do nothing else. What are these femmes fatales doing today? Are they off to the post office for their pensions or are they strolling along Hollywood Boulevard? If you recognise one of them as your great aunt Lucy, ask her why she is passing rude comments about the amount of leg your miniskirt is showing. She had her moments!

Above right: The bathing beauty competition on the sands attracted large crowds who liked to guess whether their opinion matched that of the judges. Bournemouth and other resorts organised many different types of contest. There were glamorous grannies, bouncing babies and great granddads. None could quite match the attractions of the young lovelies who paraded on the stage in their swimsuits. Women looked from the audience with a mixture of jealousy and criticism. They offered comments about bottoms being too large or hair not nicely permed, but secretly wished that they had the courage and trim figures to be up there instead. As for the men, well they just ogled and had little fantasies like they always did. This contest was sponsored by the Sunday Pictorial. It was the first picture newspaper to appear in London. It was part of the stable of papers that included the London Evening News, Daily Mail and Daily Mirror. The Pictorial aimed for a large popular readership. It was often criticised as vulgar and poorly written, but it helped make a fortune for Harold and Alfred Harmsworth, later Lord Rothermere and Lord Northcliffe. Their newspaper empire featured short articles written in simple, exciting language. They featured sensational stories and highlighted scandals. All their publications relied heavily on photographs. Many of those enjoying the contest pictured were their readers. The Sunday Pictorial brought stimulating pictures to its clientele. What was more attractive to the eye than the sight of the Bournemouth belles who paraded that day?

Movie star Marilyn Monroe was one of the top box office draws of the 1950s. In such films as 'Gentlemen Prefer Blondes' and 'The Seven Year Itch', her glamorous and sexy style was just the thing to perk us up in our ordinary lives that were just emerging from the austerity of the postwar era. Britain tried to find its own stars to rival her. Diana Dors and Joan Collins found some success, but neither could rival Norma Jean, as she was really called. Pop composer Elton John even rewrote his song about her, 35 years after her death, as a tribute to Diana, Princess of Wales. Monroe's name was the inspiration behind the launching of a magazine called 'Marilyn' in Britain. Down on Bournemouth beach, the Sunday Pictorial was clever enough to use all this to try to bring something a bit different from the run of the mill bathing beauty contest. Rather than just the usual parade of girls in swimsuits, holding their entry numbers at their sides, they were persuaded to check out their vital statistics. Marilyn's shape appeared as a cardboard cutout and the contestants got credit for how well their figures matched those of the movie queen. The Sunday Pictorial was a popular newspaper of the period. Part of the Northcliffe empire, begun by the Harmsworth brothers, it was first published in March 1915 as a sister to the Daily Mirror. It was renamed the Sunday Mirror in 1963.

The bluebirds were flying over the white cliffs of Dover and above Pokesdown, Stourcliff and Westbourne as well. Glad hearts rejoiced at the news that the war in Europe had come to an end. Our boys would soon be on their way home. It was time to show the flag, literally. The Square was festooned with red, white and blue. Union Jacks were pulled out of cupboards. They had lain there since the coronation of George VI. The mixture of relief and excitement bonded everyone together, just as the dark days of the war had seen communities work for each other. Marching bands and ranks of the armed services would make their way past the cheering crowds and the 'great' could be put back into Britain once more. There was still a lot of work to do to get back on our feet, but that was for tomorrow. Today was for celebration. Afterwards, the flags would be furled away, but would return

in force a few months later when Japan surrendered. Central to the scene is Bobby's department store. It dominated the southwest end of the Square and was one of the top shops in the town. In the mid 19th century, Poole was the main shopping area, but, gradually, Bournemouth became self sufficient in this respect. The first clutch of shops appeared around the Square and then spread to Commercial Road and, later, along Old Christchurch Road. Bobby's became Debenham's, but some locals still call it by the old name.

Events of the 1950s

WHAT'S ON?

Television hit Britain in a big way during the 1950s. Older readers will surely remember 'Double Your Money, Dixon of Dock Green and 'Dragnet' (whose characters' names were changed 'to protect the innocent'). Commercial television was introduced on 22nd September 1955, and Gibbs SR toothpaste were drawn out of the hat to become the first advert to be shown. Many believed adverts to be vulgar, however, and audiences were far less than had been hoped for.

GETTING AROUND

The year 1959 saw the development of the world's first practical air-cushion vehicle - better known to us as the hovercraft. The earliest model was only able to travel at slow speeds over very calm water and was unable to carry more than three passengers. The faster and smoother alternative to the sea ferry quickly caught on, and by the 1970s a 170-ton car-carrying hovercraft service had been introduced across the English Channel.

SPORTING CHANCE

The four-minute mile had remained the record since 1945, and had become regarded as virtually unbreakable. On 6th May 1954, however, Oxford University student Roger Bannister literally ran away with the record, accomplishing the seemingly impossible in three minutes 59.4 seconds. Bannister collapsed at the end of his last amazing lap, even temporarily losing his vision. By the end of the day, however, he had recovered sufficiently to celebrate his achievement in a London night club!

The Square is situated at the heart of Bournemouth's shopping area. From here roads lead off in all directions and it was once full of traffic crawling across it. These days it is pedestrianised and contains attractive mosaics and brickwork. There are large department stores within easy reach and the Square is now a place where street players come to entertain passers-by. It is also a popular place to meet friends, as it was in 1945 when this scene across the tram shelter towards Richmond Hill was captured. The building on the right is that of the NatWest bank. The bunting and flags were being strung up in readiness for the VE celebrations. Nearly six years of hostilities had come to an end and we were going to party as never before. Trestles would be

dragged out onto the streets and neighbourhoods would combine to have the shindig of all time. In the town centre there would be processions and speeches, with services in all the churches and celebrations in the parks. The shelter had a thermometer mounted on it. On it could be seen the progress towards the national and local targets set for fund raising as part of the war effort. There were drives to raise money for tanks, aeroplanes and warships. The shelter has been replaced by the Camera Obscura, a contraption that is supposed to give periscope like views across the town. Tables and chairs for people taking refreshments now stand near where the trams stopped. The clock, with a little fish on top, is the only remnant of this building.

Bottom: Mixed in with the celebrations for regatta week, the children's sections have always played a large part. Whilst teams of athletes were pitting their skills against each other in the sculls and on the yachts, there were gentler competitions being held. These attracted the less physical amongst us. We could not all tack into the wind or heave on a mighty oar. Some were happier to follow more artistic pursuits. They wanted to stretch their imaginations and delicacy of touch, rather than rippling biceps. In the summer of 1939, there was a nautical feel to the handicraft section of the art competition in which these children were exhibiting their models. One little lad even joined in the spirit of the day by donning his best sailor suit. Others appeared in their cub uniforms or school clothes. Boys often appeared at public functions with blazers, ties and caps proudly showing off their school loyalty. What pride does modern youth show by turning up in jeans and trainers? Does that not send out a message? The girls put on pretty frocks and little white ankle socks. Not for them the Armani outfits or Stella McCartney designs their grandchildren would demand before setting foot outside the house. Much cutting, glueing and shaping had gone into the preparation of these works of art the kiddies put on show. They all deserved a prize for their efforts. Pity the poor judge who had to choose a winner. Let us hope she chose one that was the child's own work and not one heavily influenced by mum's contribution.

Right: Nobody sleeps when we are on. This could have been the band's motto. There must have been around 50 assorted trombones, cornets, bugles and trumpets belting out a number on this march. We love a good brass band and the power of the instruments is somehow reassuring. Even when baby is woken up by the blast from a euphonium, we almost forgive the bandsmen completely. It is such good old British sound that makes you glad to be alive, even if a bit deafened. When the church band comes around the streets at Christmas, the lovely sound of Christmas carols can bring a lump to the throat. The local Boscombe Salvation Army Band is one of the country's best. Formed in 1886, it has played at the Royal Albert Hall and Wembley. The band travels around the various Bournemouth bandstands during the summer months. It has been giving these regular public concerts for over half a century since it first began the custom in 1946. At first, Fisherman's Walk, Sherbourne was home to the band. In the 1990s, a base was set up at Pine Walk, in Bournemouth's lower pleasure gardens. National TV audiences have heard the music of the Boscombe Salvation Army Band, even if they did not realise it. These followers of General Booth played the theme music for actress Dame Thora Hird's 'Praise be' series. It is an army whose war cry is limited to the title of its magazine.

Above: The end of regatta week was marked with a magnificent firework display. Cynics always said that the start of the week always meant that rain was due and that the fireworks were the sign that the sunny weather was about to begin. Looking down from West Cliff, the pier is lit up like a beacon. The floodlights illuminated the scene and twinkling pinpricks gleamed out like so many fireflies in the night. Overhead, the rockets whooshed and Roman candles spat their glowing fireballs into the night sky. Crowds that gathered to enjoy the show oohed and aahed at the spectacle. Drops of colour fell from the sky as the sparks from the fireworks returned to earth. You had to be quick to catch everything. One turn of the head and you could see another starburst, but miss the whiz of the next set of Catherine wheels spinning behind you.

The best of it all was to look at the faces of the young children who had come to witness the celebrations. In their eyes you could see the magic of the occasion. In their open mouths was the wonder that only the young can bring to these sorts of events. We had seen it all before, but for the tots this was something not to be missed. If we would just admit it, even the grumpiest of us could not help but share some of the excitement of the time.

Top: People gathered on top of the cliff to get a good look down at the pier. Regatta week was rounded off with a grand ball and firework display. All around them the spectators marvelled at the riot of colour being thrown into the night sky. The crackle of the exploding fireworks and the smell of burning gunpowder were sights, sounds and smells that roused the senses. They stayed in the memories of the watchers for weeks to come. The display of pyrotechnics goes back to ancient China for its origins. The idea developed from the military rockets and explosive missiles that were actually used in the very first such displays. The risks to life and limb from these soon led their being scaled down into less dangerous and more manageable modern fireworks. Even these are still the source of injury and, on occasion, death today, despite greater precautions being taken. It was the 19th century that brought the addition of new ingredients. Magnesium and aluminium greatly heightened the brilliance of such displays. The spectators at West Cliff did not worry about the chemical content of the fireworks. There may have been potassium nitrate, sulphur and charcoal in the thunderflashes and potassium chlorate and metal salts combining to create the wondrous colours, but they did not care for the analysis. They just wanted to share the sense of childlike wonder that even the biggest 'seen it - done it' cynic was showing that summer evening.

Left: Meyrick Park is home to a golf club that was opened by Mrs George Meyrick in 1894. Those were the days when golfers carried mashie niblicks and wooden spoons in their bags. They were a far cry from the carbon fibre tackle of today. The park itself, situated in an area bordered by the railway line to the north and the Bourne Stream to the south, has been the centre for jamborees, girl guide gatherings, fetes, carnivals, celebrations and any number of other large gatherings. The 1889 Bournemouth Park Laws Act decreed that Meyrick Park should be set aside for the enjoyment and recreational use of the public. FW Lacey laid out the park and Tom Dunn designed the golf links. In 1902, crowds celebrated the coronation of Edward VII. They would return for successive monarchs. Memorial services were held here after the two world wars. Another notable gathering came in 1999 when the Countryside Alliance met to protest at the government's attitude towards the rural community. This coincided with the Labour party conference at the BIC. Here the large crowd has gathered to listen to the music of the band. Maybe it was playing some of the songs from the shows of the day, 'Oklahoma' or 'Annie get your gun'. Elsewhere, families walked in the sunshine and thought about what the early postwar years promised. The NHS was born and the prime minister, Clement Attlee, said we would have greater social equality. The trouble was that we knew the world was still an unhappy place. Communism was a threat to peace. There was unrest in Palestine and on the Indian subcontinent.

Below: We need a central point to grieve and remember. All over the world, tribes and races get together in public displays of sorrow and remembrance. In the western world we use cenotaphs and memorials to provide a meeting place for occasions when we recall the passing of those who have served us and whom we have loved. Bournemouth's cenotaph is to be found in the upper pleasure gardens off Bourne Avenue. Unlike some, it does not hit you in the face as you walk around the town centre. Whilst not hidden, it is discreetly placed near the town hall and Richmond Hill United Reform Church. On Remembrance Sunday every village, parish, town and city has assemblies to recall the sacrifice of those brave men and women who fell in defence of this land. The Lord Lieutenant of Hampshire, General J Seely (later Baron Mottistone), unveiled this memorial on 8 November 1922. It was sculpted by WA Hoare from a design by EA Shervey. Constructed in Portland stone, it survived Goering's bombers that dropped their explosive loads on the town during World War II. One bomb came close. It landed just 30 yards away. Although the cenotaph was covered in mud, it remained intact. In September 1997 the area was covered with floral tributes to the popular Princess of Wales, who died in a car crash on 31 August. For all those honoured here we say, 'Lest we forget.'

Events of the 1950s

HOT OFF THE PRESS
The 1950s seemed to be the heyday of spies, and in 1951 the activities of Guy Burgess and Donald Maclean caused a sensation in the country. Both had occupied prominent positions in the Foreign Office, while Burgess had also been a member of MI-6. Recruited by the Russians while at Cambridge University in the 1930s, the traitors provided the Soviets with a huge amount of valuable information. They disappeared in 1951, surfacing in Moscow five years later.

THE WORLD AT LARGE
Plans to develop the economies of member states into one common market came to fruition on 1st January 1958, when the EEC came into operation. The original members were France, Belgium, Luxembourg, The Netherlands, Italy, and West Germany. The Community became highly successful, achieving increased trade and prosperity across Western Europe while at the same time alleviating fear of war which lingered on after the end of World War II. Britain became a member in 1973.

SCIENCE AND DISCOVERY
DNA (deoxyribonucleic acid) was first defined as long ago as 1953, and the effects have been far-reaching. The key discovery was developed over the following years and today DNA fingerprinting has become an accepted part of life. Genetic diseases such as hemophilia and cystic fibrosis have been identified. Criminals are continually detected and brought to justice. Biological drugs have been developed. More controversially, drought and disease-resistant plants have been engineered - and Dolly the sheep has been produced.

Coming along Exeter Road on the way up to Bath Road, the streets are lined with people watching the carnival floats and listening to the marching band. Pride of place in the parade has gone to the carnival queen. Such events would not see people turn out in force these days. Fifty years ago, the regatta and carnival was a grand affair. We had little to cheer during the war years, so it was good to get out and enjoy simple British pleasures once again. Society today has gained a lot,

but some of the good things of yesterday have been lost. The sense of community, when we openly rejoiced in being the folk of Bournemouth, has taken a back seat. The queen was lucky for the sun shone on her. The committee could not run to a limousine, but she still got her open top tour of the town. Looking as pretty as a picture, she would remember the honour for the rest of her life. Today, sitting in her armchair, she will turn the pages of her scrapbook for the grandchildren and remind them of the pride she felt in her selection. Her two pretty attendants might look back on the day with a tinge of envy that they were not the centre of attraction. But, there would have been other days for them, we are sure. The day was bright and it matched the mood of the occasion.

Above: JE Beale was long gone by the time of the 1954 Christmas procession. His store still supported the parade. As well as being a gift to the town, it marked the start of Christmas shopping week. At least the period did not begin as soon as Easter eggs were finished, as it seems to nowadays. Beale felt he had to put something back into the town for the success it had given him. In the 1914-18 war he had worked tirelessly, raising funds for the war effort. He helped the Belgian refugees who came to Bournemouth. For this he received the Medaille du Roi Albert and the Russian Cross. Family members continued his links with the town council. Throughout the 20th century there always seemed to be a Councillor Beale in office. Beale's began to provide the Christmas procession in 1885. There cannot have been as many imaginative and amusing figures as the cellos of 1954. Look carefully at their eyes. Each one has a slightly different squint from the other members of the string section. Bournemouth people looked forward every year to this display of fun and festivity. There was a public outcry when the custom was abandoned in 1988. A tradition dating back over 100 years disappeared and many were not best pleased. Beale's spent the money it used to give to the parade on decorations, trees and Christmas lights instead. Santa still appears, but, sadly, the cross-eyed cellos have fiddled away to nothing.

Above right: The Regent Cinema was on Westover Road, opposite the Pavilion. It was a building designed by WE Trent. The Regent became the Gaumont in 1949. Since 1986 it has been called the Odeon. Father Christmas drove past, looking a very important figure flanked by his footman and coachman, on his way to do his duty by the good girls and boys of Bournemouth. He was kind enough to include some of the naughty ones, as well. That winter's day, in late 1947, the Regent was showing 'I Love Trouble'. It starred Franchot Tone. He was a popular leading man of the day. Born in 1905, he had starred in such major Hollywood epics of the 1930s as 'Lives of a Bengal Lancer' and the 1935 production of 'Mutiny on the Bounty'. He was married four times. The most notable of these was his marriage to Joan Crawford (1935-39). Tone died in 1968. Father Christmas was not interested in old movie stars. He was the linchpin of the Christmas procession that drew people onto the streets every year as part of a gift to the community from Beale's. By the beginning of the 20th century, the department store had developed from its fancy fair origins. It sold clocks, tableware, toiletware and books, whilst retaining some flavour of the old days. The founder served the community on a personal basis by becoming active in the church and town council. He was also a Justice of the Peace.

Below: As the 1955 Christmas procession turned the corner of Bath Road and Exeter Road, children in the crowd were looking forward to putting up their own stockings on Christmas Eve. Sometime during the night, Father Christmas called and the little ones would think how marvellous it was that he had managed to fit in all his calls. They also remarked that Santa sometimes left the price tags on, but did not let this oddity bother their sense of mystery. Fortunately, they did not catch the accusing glance that mum shot across at dad. In 1969, it was decided to pedestrianise this part of the road when plans to build the flyover were made. It came into being in 1972. JE Beale, founder of the procession's sponsor, would have enjoyed the fancy scene. He had run a business known as the fancy fair. He had a difficult upbringing as his father was lost at sea when he was a boy. Renting a shop near Old Christchurch Road, adjoining the Arcade, he began with a small capital of £400. His fancy fair sold fancy goods to the less wealthy holiday-makers and working classes. At first, his wife ran the business, as he could not gain release from his employer in Weymouth. When the Beales eventually joined forces, trade expanded quickly. The coming of the railway helped this. It brought visitors in large numbers and money into the tills of the fancy fair.

I saw three ships come sailing in, on Christmas day, on Christmas day. On Christmas day in the morning. The Nina, Pinta and Santa Maria were the ships in Columbus' little fleet that set off in 1492 on the voyage of discovery to the Americas. In the Christmas song they became vehicles for the baby Jesus. On Bath Road they were part of the annual procession that thrilled thousands of spectators who turned out in the winter to chill to enjoy the start of the Christmas period. In other parades they would see giant puddings, turkeys and caterpillars as the organisers of the procession came up with different ideas to amuse and entertain the public. Some of the crowd wrapped up in duffel coats, the new style of warm overcoat that had become popular. A particular fad of the young, these coats fastened with little plastic or wooden toggles that were a nightmare for small children to undo. They became the standard wear for students. The coat was named after the Belgian town where these hooded garments first saw the light of day. The procession was sponsored by Beale's store that still occupies a prominent place in the town centre. Sometimes, part of Old Christchurch Road is called Beale's corner, so well known has the store become. It was founded by John Elmes Beale. He was born in Weymouth in 1849, where he was apprenticed to a draper. He died in 1928.

Duffel coats were named after the small Belgian town where they were first worn

On the move

Below centre: There is no truth in the rumour that diehard socialists erected this sign, wishing that new Labour would revert to its old ways. The Bournemouth International Centre hosts many political party conferences, but this scene dates to a time when the BIC was not even a twinkle on the horizon. Maybe it was an indicator for Lewis Tregonwell, back in 1810, to take notice of the land he was passing by. If so, it is a good job he did. Without him, there might have been no Bournemouth. He was a Dorsetshire squire and army captain in charge of coastal defences during the period 1796-1802. He and his wife were staying at Muddiford, near Christchurch, when they decided to explore Bourne Mouth and the chines. She fell in love with the place and got Lewis to build a summer residence so that they could indulge in the new fad of sea bathing. Lewis Dymoke Grosvenor Tregonwell, to give him his full name, built what was to become Exeter House. In 1814, he added more land above Cranborne Road to his estate. By his death, in 1832, his holdings were extensive. He had land on both sides of Exeter Road, including a triangular piece drawn from Yelverton Road, Old Christchurch Road and Richmond Hill. The Tregonwells also built a number of houses to augment the mansion they had erected for themselves and the settlement at the mouth of the Bourne was to become the town we know today. Thank you for your left turn, Lewis and Henrietta.

Bottom: Turning the corner at Fir Vale Road from Old Christchurch Road, the bus is close to an area that is now a pedestrianised shopping area. The road on which Timothy White's stood took its name from the estate known as the Firs that once covered much of this area and that to the south. Firs Cottage and the Grand Fir Vale Hotel used to stand further along this road. The ugly overhead cables have now gone, as have the trolley buses that used to carry passengers into town. The sparks no longer fly from the pantographs that reached greedily skywards to suck their electrical lifeblood from above. At the start of the 20th century you could see trams operating around here. Although an efficient means of public transport, restricted movement on their tracks meant some congestion being created on the streets as the numbers of other road users grew. The Bournemouth Corporation Act of 1930 saw the introduction of trolley buses as an experiment. The scheme took off. As they proved very popular and were more flexible in their movements than the old tramcars, the days of the tram were numbered. Eventually, the trolley bus disappeared as well. It fell victim to the criticism of causing jams that had been levelled at the trams. There was a sort of poetic justice in this. There is now little evidence to be found in or around the town that either form of transport ever existed.

The Royal Bath Hotel stands high above East Cliff Promenade, looking down at the pier walk below. The distinctive pointed cornices of its roof can be seen from most parts of the bay. They have acted as a welcome to the boats approaching the pier and as a backdrop for their leaving throughout the 20th century. There is no reason why the skyline should change in the 21st. In 1949 there was a more laid back feel to life, compared to what we had suffered a few short years before. The task of rebuilding our lives after the war was well under way. A more relaxed mood was in the air and we were looking beyond the austerity of the present day to prosperity that surely would follow. We were optimistic and the feeling was represented by the casual body language of the sailors and their clients. Although the ferry service to Swanage had to be discontinued because of the deterioration of its pier,

Bournemouth continued to flourish. Improvements to the pier continued to be made, as they had in the past. The installation of electric light in 1899 was one of the indications that the town recognised the pier's importance in the growth of the resort into a position of some importance. The landing stage extension was opened in 1909. No less a figure than the Lord Mayor of London, Sir George Wyatt Truscott, was invited to wield the ceremonial scissors. A new entrance was built in 1929 and the solarium added in 1934.

Events of the 1950s

MELODY MAKERS

Few teenage girls could resist the blatant sex-appeal of 'Elvis the Pelvis', though their parents were scandalised at the moody Presley's provocatively gyrating hips. The singer took America and Britain by storm with such hits as 'Jailhouse Rock', 'All Shook Up' and 'Blue Suede Shoes'. The rhythms of Bill Haley and his Comets, Buddy Holly and Chuck Berry turned the 1950s into the Rock 'n' Roll years.

INVENTION AND TECHNOLOGY

Until the late 1950s you did not carry radios around with you. Radios were listened to at home, plugged into a mains socket in every average sitting room. Japan was in the forefront of electronic developments even then, and in 1957 the Japanese company Sony introduced the world's very first all-transistor radio - an item of new technology that was small enough to fit into your pocket. The major consumer product caught on fast - particularly with teenage listeners.

ROYAL WATCH

King George VI's health had been causing problems since 1948, when he developed thrombosis. In 1951 the King - always a heavy smoker - became ill again, and was eventually found to be suffering from lung cancer. His left lung was removed in September of 1951. In January 1952 he waved Princess Elizabeth and Prince Philip off on their tour of Africa; they were never to see him again. The King died in the early hours of 6th February 1952.

Above: It is all right for some. Whilst others scurry along the pier to catch the ferry or throw out painters to secure the steamer to the jetty, this deck chair potato is in a world of his own. Maybe he was reminiscing about the history of the paddle steamer that had hove into view. The Emperor of India was one of a fleet of such craft that were a common sight off the south coast. Originally built as a 428 ton, 195 feet steel hulled ship in 1906 by Thorneycroft of Southampton, it was first known as the Princess Royal. Two years later, having been lengthened by 22 feet and increasing to 482 tons, it was sold to Cosens and renamed. During the first world war it served as a troopship, floating hospital and minesweeper. A popular pleasure steamer in the early 20s, it was leased to Brighton during 1922. The Emperor of India again saw active service in the 40s as a minesweeper and ack-ack ship on the Thames and as a training vessel on the Clyde. By 1948 it was back in harness in Bournemouth, having been refitted as a 534 tonner capable of carrying 800 passengers. It continued its usefulness until 1956, being sold to Belgium for scrap in 1957. By 1959, its hull was being used as an Antwerp theatre. In 1915, the Consul served in the Dardanelles. In the 1950s it sailed to Weymouth and Lulworth Cove. It ceased to operate in 1962. The Empress was a film star, appearing in the 1946 movie, 'Great Expectations'. Other ships of the postwar period included the Lorna Doone II, Monarch and Embassy.

Right: Steamships first called at the pier in 1860. By the end of the century, south coast steamers were in their heyday. In 1898 no fewer than 44 of them plied their trade along this stretch of the Channel. They continued to be a force through the first half of the next century, but, after the second world war, their influence dwindled. By 1959 only 16 remained in service. Just half a dozen of the historic paddle steamers were included in this number and the end of the halcyon days was nigh. As the 21st century began, not all contact with the old days had been lost. Boat trips on the likes of the Dorset Belle could still be had to Swanage, Poole Harbour, Isle of Wight and the Dorset Lakes. This view of the town, dating from 1949, shows an array of hotels and guesthouses that abound the coastline. Bournemouth had grown from virtually nothing to a flourishing town in a relatively short time. In the early 1800s it was just a collection of estates, governed from rural Holdenhurst. By 1856, an administrative area of 1,140 acres had been established around the Belle Vue Hotel. This was probably the first recognised stirring of Bournemouth as a small town, though its main services were centred in Christchurch. The town hall did not come along until as recently as 1921. The Mont Dore Hotel, built in 1885, had served this purpose until then. By the end of the millennium the population had risen to about 160,000.

SKYLARK 6
SKYLARK 3

Left: All aboard the Skylark. Generations of adults will remember that call by Nutty Noah and Nelly from their days watching children's TV in the 70s. But, Bournemouth was ahead of its time. To be more precise, it was a memorable local character who immortalised the Skylark for all residents and visitors. Jake Bolson, nicknamed the 'prince of the seas', inherited from his father a handful of rowing boats that he used to rent out to holidaymakers. Jake built the business into one with a large fleet of motor boats and a boat building concern. His famous Skylark fleet carried tourists around and across the bay on excursions and fishing trips. In between the two world wars and into the 1950s 'all aboard the Skylark' made Jake a popular figure. So much success and pleasure did he get from his enterprise that he named his home Skylark Nest. He built his own jetty in 1947 for use with the Skylarks. It was removed in 1976. Jake served in World War I on minesweepers and was also a member of the secret service. His boats were not limited to those pictured here. His yard was responsible for the famous Bournemouth Belle and the pleasure yacht, Titlark. Despite his success, he never lost touch with normality. When his beloved dog died, the flags on the Skylarks flew at half mast. On a more important note, he helped organise lifesaving off the Bournemouth coast and a collection for the sufferers of the 1952 Lynmouth flood disaster. He died in 1953, aged 64, and was buried on a stormy day with thunder and lightning marking his passing. His son, Dick, carried on the business.

Above: The two funnel paddle steamer releases its load of passengers onto the eastern jetty at the side of the pier. From there it is but a short climb to the main pier and then it is onward, down its length, and off into the town. This was a scene that had been commonplace in the 1920s and 1930s, but had not long returned to the normal pattern of life by 1947. After the Great War a number of the ships that had served the area well had been left to rot at anchorage. This sad waste was made up for by the ones that returned from war duties to ply their trade once more, ferrying passengers along Poole Bay to Swanage or across to the Isle of Wight. After the second world war, people were anxious to reuse the services and get back to normal. The days of many of the vessels were, unfortunately, numbered. A flurry of nostalgia helped keep the boats afloat for a while in the late 40s and early 50s. Such steamers as the Bournemouth Queen, built in 1908, had seen active service in both the major wars. In the 1914-18 conflict she was known as HMS Bourne and had served as an anti aircraft ship in the Firth of Forth during the 1939-45 period. Passengers were happy to mark her noble record by boarding her on the run to Swanage, but she was soon to find that time was running out. In 1951 she moved to the Southampton service and was scrapped in 1957.

Fun & games!

The obstacle races are being run on the beach. There are sack races and egg and spoon events to come. Ice cream vendors are encouraging the crowds to buy a cornet or wafer and to choose whether or not to have a dab of raspberry on top. There are toffee apples being eaten, at great risk to youngsters' teeth as they bite into the hard, sticky coating. Sometimes they got more than they bargained for. Just once in a while, there was a little extra wiggling around inside the apple. Ugh! Remember finding a grub in there? You never forgot taking a bite and only discovering half of one. That really turned your stomach! Never mind, what is exciting the crowds at this moment is the sight of the boats arriving. Regatta week is well under way and, in the late 1930s, it was an event that grabbed the attention of everyone on the foreshore and up on the pier. Soon they would be launched and the sea racing begin. In its heyday, the regatta was a week of fun, packed with all manner of things. Serious competition mixed happily with the lighter element. The lifeguards showed their skill in challenges against other teams. There were talent contests, glamorous granny and grandest granddad judging, miss and master tiny tot events and bonnie baby parades. Bathing beauties were on show and there were plastic duck races on the Bourne. Locals met the challenge of walking the greasy pole and, in later years, there were BMX bike races and a fly past from the Red Arrows. It all came to a conclusion in the grand ball.

Above: As an island race, the British have always had a fascination for the water. The British Navy once ruled the world's waves and our merchant fleet brought us prosperity in overseas trade. In our recreational periods we love 'messing about in boats'. Whether it was on the Thames at Henley, the Norfolk Broads or pottering around a boating lake, no matter. We could all be Nelsons for a day. Why else would the Oxford v Cambridge boat race still feature as one of the TV sporting attractions of the year? Few of us have any connection with either university, but the riverbanks are lined and the TV lounges filled every year. Some of our best sporting achievements have come on the water. That magnificent rower, Stephen Redgrave, brought home four gold medals from different Olympics in the 1980s and 1990s. Bournemouth people enjoyed the annual regatta. Established in 1869, the regatta committee had continued to administer the event until 1914 when it was disbanded with the outbreak of war. A fetes and entertainment committee was then formed in 1917, amalgamating with the sports' committee a year later, at the end of the war. The regatta committee that took over the full organisation of all the events and activities came together in 1939. In this photograph you can see the peaked caps and commodore style hats of rowing and sailing fans. The starting gun has boomed and the coxed fours race is well under way.

Top: Crews are preparing to launch their boats as they get ready to compete in one of the many races that made up regatta week. Followers of the sport will know that the team members who use one oar each, rather than a pair, are more properly said to be sculling. They hoped for a calm day on which to participate. A strong swell made pulling across the sea difficult. Launching the craft was an art in itself, with breaking waves to be negotiated without being swamped before even getting under way. Any number of rowing clubs could be found in the area. One such was the Westover club. It had been formed by the amalgamation of the Bournemouth Bicycle and Westover Rowing Clubs. The rowing club held its inaugural dinner in 1871. This exhausting sport was only for the fittest and strongest. In the early days, the rowing club members used to put their galley on a pair of trucks. Then it was trundled along to the local regattas at neighbouring Christchurch and Poole. They must have been out of puff before they got started. The softies of later years had lorries and trailers to make life easier. Other club members are seen here helping with the preparations. Older rowers, whose best days were behind them, were always keen to pass on their experience and a few tips about the conditions. The current team usually smiled, nodded a thank you and then did its own thing.

'Little boy fishing off a wooden pier' was a popular song that Uncle Mac used to feature regularly in Children's Favourites on the Light Programme in the 1950s. If younger readers cannot make head nor tail of that, then we are referring to a record request show on what is now BBC Radio 2. (Records were what we wrinklies had before CDs!) Uncle Mac was the presenter, DJ to you. His real name was Derek McCullough. The tune could have been written for this scene from the 1930s. Enjoying a flask of hot Bovril to keep the cockles of the heart as well as the fingers warmed, these lads are well set for a good day's sport. The problems faced by anglers are still those of their ancestors: where to find fish, how to approach them and what sort of bait to use. The angler must understand

wind and weather. Fishing remains what it has always been, a problem in applied natural history. Phew! That is an awful lot for little lads to take in. Perhaps they were not that worried. They were happy in each other's company and could enjoy the chat that went along with the fishing. By now, they will be in the golden years of their lives. Let us hope that they still share a drink, the crack and a spot of angling off Boscombe pier. 'Come fish, bite fish, swim along here.'

Events of the 1960s

WHAT'S ON?

Television comedy came into its own in the 1960s, and many of the shows that were favourites then went on to become classics. 'On the Buses', 'Steptoe and Son', 'Till Death Us Do Part' and 'The Army Game' kept audiences laughing, while the incredible talents of Morecambe and Wise, the wit of Des O'Connor - often the butt of the duo's jokes - and the antics of Benny Hill established them for ever in the nation's affections.

GETTING AROUND

The 2nd March 1969 was a landmark in the history of aviation. The Anglo-French supersonic airliner Concorde took off for the first time from Toulouse in France. Concorde, which can cruise at almost twice the speed of sound, was designed to fly from London to New York in an incredible three hours twenty minutes. The event took place just weeks after the Boeing 747, which can carry 500 passengers to Concorde's modest 100, made its first flight.

SPORTING CHANCE

Wembley Stadium saw scenes of jubilation when on 30th July 1966 England beat West Germany 4-2 in the World Cup. The match, played in a mixture of sunshine and showers, had been a nailbiting experience for players and spectators alike from the very beginning when Germany scored only thirteen minutes into the game. It was Geoff Hurst's two dramatic goals scored in extra time that secured the victory and lifted the cup for England - at last.

Left: The Bournemouth Angling Club turned out in all weathers. A bit of a blow and a spot of rain did not stop these members from casting their lines into the waters in 1933. Fishermen are made of stern stuff. It comes as no surprise to see people from this area enjoying their angling. Bournemouth, after all, was a little fishing hamlet in the 18th and early 19th century. From early records of the district it had been little more than a stretch of coastline during the Tudor period. Even those first homes were some distance from the actual mouth of the Bourne. Until the Tregonwells came here in 1810, there were no houses within three miles of there. Travellers from Christchurch to Poole crossed pen heathland, passing just the odd decoy hut used by the hunters of wildfowl. These anglers might have been able to trace their sport back to 2000 BC when ancient Egyptians fished for fun. Although we are an island race, it was not until the late 15th century that anything is recorded about Britons angling for recreational reasons. An edition of the 'Book of St Albans', published in 1496, contains a treatise on 'fishing with an angle'. But, it was with Isaak Walton's 'Compleat Angler', written in the mid 17th century, that the sport was properly chronicled and came into popularity.

Below: Sou'westers, wellies, waterproofs and balaclavas were as essential parts of equipment to the angler of the 30s as the obvious tackle of rod, reel, hook and gaff. Boscombe pier could be a windswept old place to try to cast for bass. The pier had been first mooted in 1884, but contracts were not agreed until 1888. It was private enterprise that enabled the pier to be built at a cost of £3,813. It was an attempt to raise Boscombe's profile as a rival to Bournemouth. The design was the brainchild of local man Archibald Smith. E Howell of the Waterloo Foundry, Poole, built it. At 600 feet in length, in spans of 40 feet, its wrought iron girder frame was a fine example of Victorian engineering. The boarding that these anglers are standing on is 32 feet wide. Visitors coming along the pier approach were taken with the impressive sight of the two toll houses through whose turnstiles they would pass to gain entry to the pier proper. The pier was not designed just for show. Its 120 feet by 38 feet pier head had a landing stage on either side where excursion steamships would stop. This was a time of expansion for Boscombe. The 1871 census revealed less than 300 people living in the district. By the 1880s, the separate areas of St Clement's, Boscombe Spa and the Boscombe Estate had joined forces to become one. With the added attraction of the pier and the business it helped to bring, Boscombe was ready to expand further. By 1891, it had a population of over 6,000.

Events of the 1960s

HOT OFF THE PRESS

Barbed wire, concrete blocks and a wide no-man's-land divided East from West when a reinforced wall was built right across the city of Berlin in 1961. Many East Germans escaped to the West at the eleventh hour, taking with them only the possessions they could carry. The Berlin Wall divided the city - and hundreds of family members and friends - for 28 years until the collapse of Communist rule across Eastern Europe. Who can ever forget those scenes in 1989, when ordinary people themselves began to physically tear down the hated wall?

THE WORLD AT LARGE

'One giant leap for mankind' was taken on 20th July 1969, when Neil Armstrong made history as the first man to set foot on the moon. During the mission he and fellow-astronaut 'Buzz' Aldrin collected rock and soil samples, conducted scientific experiments - and had a lot of fun jumping around in the one-sixth gravity. Twenty-one hours and thirty-seven minutes after their landing they took off again in their lunar module 'Eagle' to rejoin Apollo II which was orbiting above them, proudly leaving the American flag on the Moon's surface.

ROYAL WATCH

Princess Margaret's announcement in 1960 that she was to wed photographer Antony Armstrong-Jones (later Lord Snowdon) brought sighs of relief from her immediate family. Just five years earlier the people of Britain had sympathised as the princess bowed to public and private pressure, ending her relationship with Peter Townsend, Prince Philip's former equerry. The Church (and the Queen, as its Head) frowned on the liaison as Townsend was divorced. Her marriage to Lord Snowdon itself ended in 1978.

Where did Nigel Short learn the skills that made him a chess grand master? If it were not on the boards of Bournemouth pier, then they would still have been developed at an early age. Even if we cannot all grow up to be world championship challengers, there is still a lot to be said for playing games as youngsters, rather than wandering the streets at a loose end and getting into mischief. Even the computer games of the modern age give children an interest with which to fill empty

moments, even if they are missing out on some of the interests that we had as kids. The boy, about to make his play in this 1949 battle of strategy being fought on the pier, will be in his 60s by now. What did he make of his life? Did he use the thinking processes and mathematical skills needed to develop successful gambits in his later life? Was he to be found teaching sums to the next generation in some local primary school or was he destined for the city as a wheeler-dealer in the stock market? Both he and his opponent would have benefited in later life from the concentration and planning that went into the playing of such games in their childhood. Today these boys may have grown into the army of silver haired surfers who ride the airwaves of the internet, rather than the breakers of the Atlantic.

Above: The ladies of Meyrick Park bowling club knew a thing or two about bias. Looking mighty fine in their white uniforms and regulation hats, the bowls left their hands with unerring accuracy in pursuit of the little white jack. Finger tack or thumb bias turned those spheres of lignum vitae in a carefully calculated arc up and down each end of the green. Unlike their northern counterparts, these ladies played on a flat surface. Those from 'oop north' played their game on a crown green where the jack could be sent across the raised centre of the playing surface. The more orderly nature of the game played backwards and forwards in set lines better suited the temperaments of these matrons of Bournemouth. This was ladies' day at the club and, just like at the golf club, heaven help any male who had the courage or stupidity to try to encroach on their special reserve. Women had played an ever more important part in sport in the period in between the two world wars. They competed at athletics in the Olympic Games for the first time in 1928. Tennis players like Helen Wills Moody and Dorothy Round became household names in the 1930s. It should not have come as a shock to the men returning from the battlefield in the 1940s to discover that a change in the woman who had been building his tank or packing his parachute. She was now swinging his driver or making use of his bowls.

Above right: And still shuffleboard has not made it to the Olympics. Also called shovelboard or shoveboard, the game has been around a long time. It was popular with the 15th century English aristocracy. Played outdoors on a hard surface, paddles or shovels were used to send discs into numbered sections. There was also an indoor version of the game. Some of the great country houses had boards of exquisite workmanship; that at Chartley Hall, in Staffordshire, was over 30 feet long. Shove-ha'penny, in which a coin or disk is pushed along a polished board so that it stops between closely ruled lines, is still a popular game in English pubs. The outdoor game gained a new lease of life on the decks of ocean liners and cruise ships. Somewhat typically, the Americans formed the National Shuffleboard Association in Florida in 1931. Two years later, this game was being played on Bournemouth pier. Competitors played a match of up to 50, 75 or 100. This game of mixed doubles appears to have come to a halt whilst tactics are discussed. The section to avoid is the one at the far end of the rink. Land in there and it is 10 off your score. Only the discs that are completely inside a segment are counted. What the rules say about a disc slipping from one section to another as the liner's deck rolled on a stormy sea is not recorded. If gold medals can be given for synchronised swimming, then why not shuffleboard?

In 1588, Francis Drake was supposed to be finishing off a game of bowls before going out to deal with the Spanish Armada. In May 1939 it was a game of putting that had to be concluded before seeing to the enemy. By the beginning of September, many young men would be swapping their putters for rifles and their golf balls for grenades. The neat suits that they wore to go down to the park and enjoy a relaxing Sunday afternoon were to be put in mothballs and exchanged for military uniforms. They marched off with the same optimistic thoughts that their fathers had 25 years before. 'Back home for Christmas' was what they said. Their mothers smiled and hoped, but knew deep inside how long they had to wait before their husbands returned from that terrible war of 1914-18. Before they would be called up, there was still one last summer of peace to enjoy. Hampshire's Portsmouth soccer club had just thumped Wolves in the FA Cup Final, there was the Len Harvey-Jock McAvoy world title fight to enjoy and a new record release of a song called 'In the mood' by Glenn Miller to whistle. There were still plenty of Sundays left to practise being like Henry Cotton, the British golfing star of the age. But, when they had passed, would come Sunday, 3 September and the words of Neville Chamberlain, 'this country is now at war with Germany. We are ready.' So were the golfers of Bournemouth.

TL
SUGAR

Left: Not so much a case of roll out the barrel as roll through it. These lads are competing in the obstacle race held as part of the children's beach sports in regatta week. It is unlikely that we are looking at the winner of the race. The heads in the crowd are all turned to the left. Presumably, the leaders are well off to the right and the boys in view are going to be hard pressed to catch them. Their parents will tell them not to worry; it was the taking part that was important. This was the spirit of the true blue Corinthian talking. No one really believed in the saying, but it sounded good. If these eager competitors did believe what mum and dad said, they must have gone on to father those who were to play soccer, rugby or cricket for England in the 1990s. That was a decade when we really did play the game for its own sake, because we never won anything! The regatta, in the middle of the 20th century, was a large affair. Crowds packed the beaches to watch the sports on land and sea and the entertainments on offer throughout the week. In recent times, it has become less important. Still occurring for a week in August, it is more child orientated as a carnival. Sandcastle competitions and beach designs give it a gentler flavour.

Above: By 1871, when the third Bournemouth regatta was held, it had become known as the annual regatta. The confidence in so naming it was well placed. It grew to become one of the high spots on the town calendar. The children, in particular, looked forward to being able to show off in front of large numbers of adults. Where else could their handicrafts, musical talents and sporting abilities get such attention. The sack race took on Olympic proportions and huge Tate and Lyle sugar bags became their passport to the gold medal. These 'sackers' are probably drawing their pensions by now, but you can bet that they still have the prizes they won that day. There will be a shelf or a little corner of a cupboard top dedicated to the prowess shown on the sands of west beach. Most of the buildings above the boys' heads have now made way for the Bournemouth International Centre. Always referred to as the BIC by locals, visitors sometimes scratch their heads when told that the prime minister is speaking at the bic tonight, wondering what he is doing talking to a pen. There were five years of arguing over the worth of spending £17 million on the centre before agreement was made. This reminded historians of the eternal wrangling over the Pavilion in the early 1900s. The BIC has taken Bournemouth into the premier league of conference towns. The 4,000 seater Windsor Hall is its centrepiece. It opened in 1984.

During the second world war, the British had been starved of much live sporting entertainment. When the soccer leagues reformed and the county cricket championship resumed, there were record crowds turning out to watch the stars who had been away. Stanley Matthews and Tom Finney attracted hordes to watch them dribble down the wing. The original Brylcreem boy, Denis Compton, had a glorious summer in 1947 when he stroked over 3,000 runs and the county grounds were bursting at the seams as spectators craned their necks to see him. So keen were people to see live sport that the comparatively minor events of children's beach games during regatta week saw thousands line the shore and fill the pier. That a group of youngsters shinning up ropes, diving through barrels and scampering along the sand should be the focus of a huge crowd seems remarkable today. The games and sports were taken

very seriously. Judges and officials were on hand to make sure that obstacles were correctly negotiated and that no short cuts were taken. The idea of a regatta and its activities had been around for about 100 years when this race was being run. There had been a regatta ball at the Belle Vue Hotel in 1849 when the first suggestions were beginning to take fruit. A Poole and Bournemouth regatta was held at Westbourne. The first Bournemouth regatta was held in 1869, followed by a second the following year.

Events of the 1960s

MELODY MAKERS

The 1960s: those were the days when the talented blues guitarist Jimi Hendrix shot to rock stardom, a youthful Cliff Richard charmed the nation with his 'Congratulations' and Sandie Shaw won the Eurovision Song Contest for Britain with 'Puppet on a String'. It was the combined musical talents of a group of outrageous working-class Liverpool lads, however, who formed the Beatles and took the world by storm with music that ranged from the experimental to ballads such as 'Yesterday'.

INVENTION AND TECHNOLOGY

A major step forward was made in 1960 when the laser was invented. An acronym for Light Amplification by Stimulated Emission of Radiation, the device produces a narrow beam of light that can travel for vast distances and is focused to give enormous power. Laser beams, as well as being able to carry far more information than radio waves, can also be used for surgery, cutting, drilling, welding and scores of other operations.

SCIENCE AND DISCOVERY

When the drug Thalidomide was first developed during the 1950s it was hailed as a wonder drug which would ease the distressing symptoms of pregnancy sickness. By the early 1960s the drug's terrible side effects were being discovered, when more than 3000 babies had been born with severe birth defects. Malformed limbs, defective eyes and faulty intestines were the heart-rending legacy left by Thalidomide.

At work

How do opinion pollsters arrive at figures telling us that 20 per cent of the population prefers sliced bread? Has anyone ever asked you? There is something annoying about being stopped in the street to answer some mindless questions, but not many refuse. The British are usually too polite. Some of us are disappointed when the woman with the clipboard lets us pass by without giving a second glance. What is wrong with me? Why do I not fit the profile? At least give me the chance to be churlish and tell you what to do with that questionnaire. There was once a chap who was asked to fill in a questionnaire and he went outside and punched the doorman, but that is another story. The researcher pictured must have had a winning personality. She has quite a little group interested in helping her conduct her survey. What can she be asking? Those interviewed seem to be young adults, so it may have been that her questions had to be directed to that age group. Whatever they were, she has succeeded in delaying their walk towards the beach. The young man with the knapsack, dressed in the baggy trousers of the day and the requisite sports jacket of the smart tourist, politely waits his turn. Soon he will be able to say that he was one of the 79 per cent of under 30 year olds who thought Bournemouth was a spiffing place to spend a holiday. Either that or he was one of the 45 per cent of young people who cracked their boiled eggs at the little end.

Respect, compassion and a sympathetic service

The Scott family has been firmly rooted in Bournemouth for well over a hundred years and the family business George Scott & Son, a funeral directing company, has been in existence for over a century.

George Henry Scott was the first member of the family to arrive in Bournemouth. He came to the town some time between 1860 and 1870 and set up his business at the Lansdowne, purchasing a house in the Square sited approximately where Debenhams can be found today. George Scott was, in his own way, a pioneer and claimed two firsts in the history of Bournemouth - he became the first part-time employee of the Bournemouth Board of Governors (which later became Bournemouth Corporation) and, with the title of 'Road Foreman', he was instrumental in bringing the first steam-roller to the town.

George's son, William Scott, was involved in the furniture industry; he moved to Boscombe and opened an upholstery and furniture business in Palmerston Road. George Henry Robert Scott, George's grandson, was also involved in the furniture industry and it was he who founded what was to become the family business, George Scott & Son. After his marriage to Annie Hannam, George and his wife moved to Somerset Road in Boscombe where, in 1899, George set up his own business and so the family company was established - in the first instance as cabinetmakers as well as funeral directors.

George worked hard during the early 1900s to develop his business. It was, however, the Great War of 1914 - 1918 that had the greatest effect on the business in its early years. A tragic aspect of this war's futile slaughter was that some of the wounded were sent to Bournemouth for treatment and convalescence and many died. George Scott & Son were selected to arrange all the resulting military funerals, with the ironic consequence of enlarging the business and making it better known.

Above left: *George Henry Robert Scott, founder of the company.*
Below: *The cortege outside Somerset Road, circa 1905.*

The decade after the war saw the first link formed in the chain of father and son in George Scott & Son that has lasted till the present day. In 1928 George's son, Harold George, joined his father in what now became truly a family business.

Harold married Lettice Eileen Lowther in 1937 and a son, Hugh, was born in 1938. The second world war was to come in 1939. Harold and Lettice's marriage was strong - no marriage could have been better able to cope with the particular tensions and strains placed on the family and the business in the war years. At first, because of his occupation, Harold was exempted from military service but he was eventually called up and served in the RAF in both India and Burma until 1945. Meanwhile the family business was ably run by Lettice and Harold's sister, Kathleen. As in the first world war, the second resulted in deaths in Bournemouth. George Scott & Son were once again involved in arranging many military funerals, this time for both allied and German personnel. One notable occurrence still remembered today is the bombing of the Metropole Hotel. Tragically this bombing raid killed many members of the RAF and Royal Canadian Air Force and George Scott & Son arranged their funerals too.

An important chapter in the history of the firm closed in 1947 with the death of the founder George Henry Robert and in the new chapter that opened then Harold, Lettice and Kathleen carried on the business. In 1957 George Scott & Son reached a turning point in the company history. Due to the increasing success of the funeral side of the business Harold decided to close the furniture side and concentrate solely on funerals.

In 1965, yet another generation of the Scott family decided to join the family business. Hugh Scott, Harold Scott's elder son, joined his father in running the company. Somerset Road had been the site used

Left: *Harold George Scott. 1907 - 1982*
Below: *1940s - RAF Funeral - Boscombe Cemetery.*
Bottom: *1927 - Scout Masters Funeral.*

by the Scotts to make their own coffins until the 1970s. However, after Hugh joined his father in the business, a new set of garages was built and six individual Chapels of Rest were added to the premises at 13-15 Somerset Road. This expansion allowed the business to continue to thrive.

Sadly in 1982 Harold George Scott, the founder's son, died. This left his son Hugh to take over and carry sole responsibility for the business built up by his father and grandfather. Hugh, therefore, became Managing Director of the Company and was assisted in its running by his wife Judith.

Only four years after his appointment as Managing Director Hugh opened a new branch office of George Scott & Son at 1537 Wimborne Road, Kinson. Hugh had seen the Kinson and Northbourne areas expand rapidly during the post-war years and decided there was a need for a funeral director in the area. The continuing success of the business after Hugh took over in 1982 meant that this expansion was possible and the new branch, with a staff member in attendance during working hours, was opened in the September of 1986.

In 1989 Hugh and Judith's second son, Neil, joined his parents in the family business. In doing so he became the fourth generation of the Scott family to continue the tradition of working for George Scott & Son.

George Scott & Son have steadily grown into one of the area's leading independent family firms. This was demonstrated in 1991 when the business expanded yet again, opening a third branch in Charminster Road, Bournemouth. To celebrate the opening of the new office, George Scott & Son joined the Golden Charter scheme enabling clients to make reassuring arrangements, including pre-payment, for their funeral.

The year 1999 was a landmark for George Scott & Son as it marked the 100th anniversary in business for the family company since its establishment in 1899. During this centenary year George Scott & Son enjoyed continuing success. The Kinson Funeral Home was extended and given an extensive refurbishment and, to mark the end of their centenary year, George Scott & Son took delivery of a new hearse and limousine. A century after the business was established, although it has seen considerable progress and expansion, the Scott family still maintain the tradition instituted by George Henry Robert Scott in 1899 - that of offering a dignified, caring, personal and comprehensive service to the people of Bournemouth and surrounding areas.

Above left: *Hugh Scott. 1938 - 1993*
Top: *1940s Humber Hearse outside Somerset Road.*

Flushed with success

Privatisation of the utility companies seems to many of us a relatively recent event. The history of Bournemouth and West Hampshire Water PLC, which charts the origins of two companies - Bournemouth Water, established 1863, and West Hampshire Water, established 1893 - shows, however, that private companies grasping the nettle (in the form, in this case, of dealing with the dangers of typhoid and cholera from contaminated water supplies) were responsible back in the nineteenth century for the establishment of good water supply practice throughout the area. To go back in time somewhat....

Try to imagine a time without running water, flushing lavatories, plumbed-in washing machines, a mains sewage system. Difficult, isn't it? Well, if you've managed to conjure up the scene, you're somewhere near to seeing the water situation as it was before the Public Health Act of 1875. Surprising as it may seem to twenty-first century citizens, obsessed as we are with hygiene in all its forms, public health prior to that date was not, to be frank, a big issue. Householders would take water from whatever well they could, without any protection from possible - even likely - contamination. The alternative was to buy water (at half an 'old' penny a bucket) from the likes of Benjamin Read who sold it from door to door. But of course, even a 'professional' like Mr Read could not, in the early years of 19th century, offer any guarantees as to the purity of his product. The situation was made much worse by another common practice at the time - disposing of the family sewage by throwing it on the garden! Over a period of time, of course, this would enter the water supply in the shallow wells used by both the likes of Mr Read and the householders themselves.

Clearly something needed to be done! It seems evident to us from this distance of time, but those innovative people offering to provide a guaranteed water supply in the early days faced a certain amount of opposition - Christchurch Council even remarking, in 1887, on the needlessness of 'hoodwinking any water company into the town'.

Above: *1894 - West Hampshire Water's first company secretary - Sambrooke Newlyn.*
Below: *Bournemouth's maintenance fitters setting off from Bourne Valley at the end of the 1800s.*

Of the two companies involved in the establishment of what is now Bournemouth and West Hampshire PLC, the Bournemouth company was the quickest off the mark - but only because William Cash - an accountant - and Edward Woods - a civil engineer, on presenting a scheme to supply gas to the town, were given a favourable response, on condition that they also provide a water supply! Consequently, in 1863, the Bournemouth Gas and Water Company was founded, on a site still used today by Southern Gas. Starting small - providing purified water to a total of six customers - the company steadily increased its client base. By 1869 there were a lucky 185 customers, safe from the perils of the evils lurking in some of the wells, and, by the time the Public Health Act was passed, the company was supplying to over 700 households. This would, of course, form a much higher proportion of the available local population than it would today.

Bournemouth was proving itself ahead of its time and the company became a statutory company, recognised by Act of Parliament in 1873. It could be said that the company was a victim of its own success in the early years, as adequate supplies were hard to maintain in the wake of increased numbers of connections, but Edward Woods continued to search for solutions to supply problems. Ill-fated projects at Tuckton and Longham village were followed by ultimate long-term success at Alderney, where a reservoir and two filters were initially built, facilitating, along with the laying of an 18 inch main, the supply of the whole area. (Ironically - in the light of the company's original objective to provide only gas to the area - the supply of gas in fact proved considerably less of a problem.)

At the beginning of the twentieth century, the problems encountered on the water front seemed to be receding - the number of reservoirs and filters at Alderney was increased, demand levelled out and the sources available were able to meet that demand. On the management front forward-looking practices were introduced - co-partnership, a system whereby each employee became a shareholder committed to working for the company for 12 months, began in 1908. In return welcome bonuses were paid to employees. Good industrial relations were further encouraged through the setting up of management/works committees. Sadly, none of these could offset the effects of the first world war, and the company suffered similar consequences to other companies of the time, losing three hundred employees for the duration.

Above left: *Steam began to replace horse-power for coal transportation in the early 1900s.*
Top: *Part of the Bourne Valley based service-laying team in the late 1800s.*

The twenties and thirties, marked as they were by the General Strike and the Depression, were similarly not particularly easy for industry in general, or the water and gas companies in particular. Demand for water continued to grow, and in 1940 powers were granted by parliament to abstract water from the River Avon - an undertaking complicated by preparations for the second world war. Work finally went ahead with the proposed work after the end of the war in 1949, but meanwhile another blow to the company's plans hovered on the horizon, in the shape of the Labour government's commitment to nationalisation.

From ½d a Bucket --

Remarkable Development of West Hampshire Water Co.

Unrivalled and Unfailing Supply

BENJAMIN READ, the funny old man whose painting dated 1841 is one of the pictures reproduced on this page, made his living by selling water from house to house in the Borough of Christchurch at ½d. a bucket. He drew his supply from a pump, dated 1732. Such was the beginning of the Christchurch Water Company!

Water at ½d. a bucket a century ago! And there was no guarantee as to its purity.

And what do we find to-day? The West Hampshire Company has spent £480,000 in constructing modern waterworks, reservoirs, and a water tower, and 300 miles of mains, while expensive pumping operations have to be carried out to take the water to the higher levels served.

What a blessing it is to have the feeling of absolute security that no matter how long a spell of drought we may have our supply of water is exhaustible for cooling drinks and refreshing baths!

And instead of paying ½d. a bucket, consumers get all the water they want on tap in their own houses at a cost of 2d. per week, where the rateable value of the cottage is £5 or less; 3d. a week where the rateable value is not over £7 10s.; and 4d. a week where the rateable value does not exceed £10. Above the £10 figure, another scale is adopted of 8% up to £15 and above that and up to £80 the charge is 7½% on the rateable value, or 1/6 in the £. There are in addition special charges.

The point to be borne in mind is the specially low charge for the smaller class houses. Every housewife realises the importance of a ready and plentiful supply of water, and it is surprising really that more of the humble homes have not taken advantage of the Company's services. Perhaps that is due to the fact that their charges are not as well known as they might be among the general public.

However, more and more houses are being connected to the mains, and it is estimated that by the end of this month—when the Company's financial year ends—approximately 1,500 additional houses will be enjoying the Company's service.

An idea of the remarkable growth of the Company is shown by the area and the population it serves, and, incidentally, these figures are indicative of the remarkable development of our Borough and district.

For instance, in Christchurch, the home of the Company, there are roughly 3,000 houses connected, and averaging 5 people to a domicile—including summer visitors—the population served in the Priory town is 15,000.

But in the section of the Borough of Lymington served by the West Hants no fewer than 3,140 houses are supplied, while if Sway and the Boldre areas are included, the total is 3,538, which on an average of five inhabitants to each house gives a population served of 17,690 people.

We do not think that it is any exaggeration to say that this total of 17,690 people reaches more than 20,000 during the summer, for Naish Farm, which is visited by thousands, is charged as one consumer, and then there is the Grand Marine Hotel, Barton, as well as several hotels in Milford, so that our Borough and district is probably the Company's largest consumer.

Here are the details of houses connected in this district: New Milton and Barton-on-Sea, 1,751; Milford-on-Sea and Pennington, 1,073; Hordle, 272; Sway, 283; Boldre, Pilley, and [illegible], 115.

About 30,000 people are served in Southbourne and Iford, 1,800 houses in Ringwood, and even Burley, Bransgore, Ripley, and Burton show their appreciation of the Company's service, no fewer than 582 houses in these four villages being served by the Company's mains. The Company goes as far north as Fordingbridge, where 137 houses are connected.

Then, the Company came to the assistance of the Borough's water undertaking when the wells failed, and provided three 3" mains services at

The West Hampshire Water Company, established a little later than its sister company, was granted its own Act of Parliament, thereby becoming a statutory company, in 1893. Christchurch, where the company had its beginnings, claims to be a place 'where time is pleasant', and indeed how much pleasanter must it have become on the founding of the company, bringing with it the availability to all of clean and uncorrupted water supplies. Several local businessmen and one London-based civil engineer, Mr Howard, met at the time with the idea of abstracting water from the River Avon, and filtering it through sand filters. A reservoir would be built on St Catherine's Hill and the water would feed back by gravity to the area of supply. The land for the reservoir was bought two years later in 1895 (two acres for two hundred pounds!), and in the same year

Above: *The gas cooker testing and spraying shop at Bourne Valley in the 1920s.*
Top: *The opening of the Christchurch works in 1895.*
Left: *An article which appeared in the New Milton Advertiser in 1937.*

the first engine driver was appointed, on trial, at the grand salary of thirty-two shillings per week (£1.60). On 13th August 1895 the Works, consisting of two triple-expansion steam engines and two Cornish boilers, were officially opened by the Fourth Earl of Malmesbury. Piped water, filtered through charcoal, was on its way to Christchurch.

By 1900 the company, despite great demand for its product, still had only three permanent employees - the secretary/manager, the engine driver and a foreman. Much work however was sub-contracted and the small number of employees does not reflect an unsuccessful venture. In 1897 increased demand led to the purchase of a new engine, new boiler, filter beds and clarifier, as well as an extension to the pumping station. At this stage agreement was reached with the Bournemouth company to take over the mains in Southbourne, as a result of which the Southbourne Water Tower was built. The area of supply continued to grow, and early in the twentieth century the New Milton Water Tower was built. By 1899, 319 of the 900 houses in Christchurch were connected to the mains supply, and builders of new houses around the old town were anxious to have supplies connected to encourage sales. Commercial customers were rapidly increasing in numbers alongside domestic clients.

The supply of water by these pioneer water companies was bound to bring some problems and, like the Bournemouth Gas and Water Company, West

Above left: *Alderney in 1895...*
Above right: *...and today.*
Below: *Poole Gas Works, Poole Quay.*

Hampshire Water faced some difficulties in the early part of the twentieth century. There were isolated complaints as to the quality of the water supplied. In a bid to lay these to rest the company chose to increase the filter beds and to sink a new well for further supplies. The water from the new well proved unsuitable for use, and despite the new filter beds the quality of the water continued to be questioned. Indeed discussion about the water quality continued for some time, not helped by the alleged personal enmity between West Hampshire's manager and the Chief Medical Officer of Health for Bournemouth.

In 1912, shortly after the appointment of a new manager/secretary, Mr David Llewellyn, at one hundred and fifty pounds per year, the company faced another crisis in the form of an outbreak of typhoid at Ringwood. Ringwood was not supplied by the company at the time, but was only 12 miles above the water intake at Knapp Mill Works. Again connections with the Bournemouth company proved useful; Southbourne mains were connected to those of Bournemouth for a short while and a chlorination plant was installed temporarily. Consequently no epidemic occurred.
Steadily both the client base and the number of employees increased. David Llewellyn had need of an assistant; an additional engine driver and boy were needed; even a telephone was deemed necessary!

It was not until 1963 that the government decided that all water resources were the nation's property

However West Hampshire also faced the perils of war. Staff were called up, including David Llewellyn, although this was later quashed due to representations made by the company. But against the odds the company managed also to find an advantage in the situation, namely the increased need for water supplies to the army camps in and around Christchurch. It is the proud boast of the company that each year since it laid its first main it has, to some degree, extended its network of operations, and the war years were no exception to this. Immediately after the first world war Knapp Mill was purchased, to enable the construction of a hydraulic turbine house to pump water to Christchurch Reservoir. Thus began a connection between the Mills family, original owners of Knapp Mill, and the West Hampshire Water Company, which still holds good today. Further developments continued with the purchase of the Royalty Fishery and the building of the Ringwood reservoir, and ultimately, after the second world war, West Hampshire found itself, like its neighbour, facing the perceived threat of nationalisation.

It was not until 1963 however that the government finally decided that all water resources were the nation's property, and water companies found themselves seeking permission to use what had

Above: *After the second world war the staff enjoy a well-deserved outing - the first for a long time.*

hitherto been regarded as their own. Under the later provisions of the Water Act of 1973, ten regional water authorities would control all aspects of water supply and management. The statutory water companies, including both West Hampshire and Bournemouth, retained their independence, but still felt the threat of nationalisation. An offensive by the statutory companies themselves eventually led to the dropping of a plan to further integrate them into the nationalised network. Politics being what it is, by 1987 the situation was completely reversed. The Conservative government of the day favoured privatisation and the statutory companies again found themselves in danger - this time from having their statutory status abolished altogether. So, far from having to worry only about the expected difficulties of water quality and excessive demand, the companies which amalgamated in 1991 to become Bournemouth and West Hampshire Water PLC, have found themselves for almost the last half century also concerned with the effects of the political situation.

But enough gloom and doom! The story of Bournemouth and West Hampshire is a success story. As a subsidiary of Biwater, the British multinational water engineering group, their aim is to place the emphasis on quality, efficiency and customer service, backed by Biwater's expertise in water supply operations.

Above: *The Bournemouth premises in the 1950s.*
Right: *George Jessel House, Alderney today.*
Below: *The Executive Management team.*

The company mission statement indicates their intention of providing a secure water supply exceeding statutory requirements at best value in an environmentally responsible manner. Their performance at attaining this level of service is well indicated by their list of proud achievements. They have the fourth lowest leakage rate of the water companies and the second lowest costs to customers. They are one of only six companies in Ofwat's 'well above average efficiency' classification. Customer complaints have reduced by approximately nine per cent. They have achieved both ISO 9001 (concerned with 'the design, development and all operations associated with the abstraction, treatment and distribution of water as a statutory undertaker, including support and customer services'), being the first water company to achieve this quality assurance accreditation. They are also the proud holders of the Investor in People award (for staff development issues)- again this was a first for a water company. And, perhaps the most impressive claim of all: they have NEVER had a hosepipe ban!

With an investment programme involving 100 million pounds between 1996 and 2005 to improve quality, reduce pollution risks and to maintain the necessary infrastructure, it is clear that this is a company which takes its obligations very seriously. They've come a long way since the days of Benjamin Read and his buckets!

One hundred years in the driving seat - and still out in front

Frederick Hendy little dreamed, when he opened his bicycle and outdoor clothing shop in Whitchurch back in 1859, that his fledgling business was destined to be the acorn from which the great oak of the Hendy Lennox Group would grow. Those, after all, were the gentle days of horsemanship, pedal power and shanks' pony, 26 years before Karl Benz invented the first petrol driven car, and nearly 50 years before Henry Ford's Model T began to roll off the assembly line.

Frederick concentrated on selling his own branded bicycles which he assembled in his shop from pre-manufactured parts. Within a short time he found that the shop was too small, and with his wife and five children he made a key move to larger premises in Southampton. The bicycle and tricycle business took off, and became a limited company in 1898. Shortly after that, Frederick diversified into four-wheeled transport, taking on agencies for Benz and Bolle - an unusual step for a bicycle dealer to take, as it was the blacksmiths and carriage builders who were making the transition to selling motor cars.

It was Frederick's son Percy who in 1910 took the bold step of signing an agreement with Henry Ford himself, making the Hendy Group the first official Ford Main Dealer in Great Britain. The Model T, or 'Tin Lizzie', lived up to Ford's - and Percy's - expectations. Hendy's also dealt in Ford commercial vehicles, and the company grew rapidly. In 1913 Hendy's opened a new branch in Palmerston Road, Bournemouth; the venture was successful and a year later another branch was opened in Southsea.

The outbreak of war brought with it a change of direction in the company, and Hendy's became responsible for the maintenance and servicing of the Fordson

***Above left:** Frederick A Hendy - founder of the company. **Below:** Palmeston Road, Bournemouth circa 1938.*

tractors, vital to the nation's food production. When peace was restored, so was the popularity of the Model T, though the price had risen steeply from £115 before the war to £220.

Between 1914 and 1938 Hendy's saw real expansion. Percy Hendy Ltd was formed in 1923, and the same year saw Frederick W Hendy appointed as company chairman, and the Bournemouth branch became the Ford Main Dealer as Hendy Bros Ltd. In Southampton the company made several moves, establishing a main headquarters, a motor-cycle and accessory showroom, a tractor sales department and a bicycle retail and wholesale venture by the name of Accessories (Southampton) Ltd. In 1938 - just a year before Britain was once more at war - a further new site was opened in Chandlers Ford, Bournemouth.

The war years were difficult ones for everyone involved in the motor trade. The Palmerston Road branch continued with truck and car servicing and also acted as a Ministry of Supply Auxiliary Workshop; meanwhile the Chandlers Ford and Vincent's Walk, Southampton branches were requisitioned by the Ministry of Aircraft Production and were used as Spitfire factories when Supermarine's factory in Northam was bombed. Hendy's had the own wartime casualties; in Southampton the Pound Tree Road building was unfortunately destroyed in an air raid.

When World War II ended in 1945 it took a number of years before the motor trade returned to normal. The launch of the new Consul and Zephyr Six at the 1950 Earls Court Motor Show marked the beginnings of a new Ford range, and these two successful models were joined by the Anglia and Prefect in 1953. By the time Hendy's celebrated their 50th anniversary in 1959 the Group was also operating as Gordon Motors in Cosham, Portsmouth - a development made in 1956 - and had extended both its Chandlers Ford and the Vincent Walk premises. When Percy Hendy died in 1956 the company passed into the hands of his nephew Arthur.

Over the following 50 years the Hendy Group grew beyond all expectations, and Hendy Ford today is established as a leading car dealership throughout the region. The tradition of success is strong within the Hendy Group; the company has proved time and again that it is quick to recognise a good opportunity and flexible enough to adapt, so although it is impossible to predict exactly what the next 50 years will bring, there can be no doubt that the Hendy Group can look forward to a bright future.

Above: *Bournemouth workshop circa 1923.*
Below: *Hendy Body, Bournemouth.*

Many a good walk has been had along the beach or cliff top since Lewis Tregonwell, acknowledged as Bournemouth's founder, first came to the area. Here we are looking from a spot close to where the modern Imax stands, with the Oceanarium to the right.

Acknowledgments

We are pleased to acknowledge the kind permission of Andrew Hawkes to reproduce photographs taken by SW Batting from the 'Bournemouth Collection of Andrew Hawkes'.

Katharine Spackman and her team at Bournemouth Reference & Local Studies Library

Thanks are also due to Andrew Mitchell who penned the editorial text and Ann Ramsdale for her copywriting skills